THE
DOWN-TO-EARTH
NATURAL FOOD
COOKBOOK

THE
DOWN-TO-EARTH
NATURAL FOOD
COOKBOOK

BY LILLIAN
LANGSETH-CHRISTENSEN

GROSSET & DUNLAP
A National General Company

Publishers   New York

Library of Congress Catalog Card Number: 72–90835
ISBN: 0-448-01362-2
First printing

Printed in the United States of America

To Andreas

CONTENTS

THE
DOWN-TO-EARTH
NATURAL FOOD
COOKBOOK

INTRODUCTION

The often-quoted statement "We are what we eat" should read "We are what we select for ourselves from the supermarket shelves and counters." Considering that American supermarkets are the best stocked in the world, it is surprising that so many of us are actually poorly nourished. Most of us select the food we eat each day without much thought about its actual relation to our well-being. We are guided by taste, convenience, and economy far more than health.

Nutrition is the science of food in its relation to our health. In view of its vital importance, we should be taught at school *what* to eat and *how* to prepare it healthfully. Instead we have to rely on the advice of books and articles, and at the moment we are understandably confused by the number of such books and the controversies that are raging. Food fads are springing up on all sides, and faddist-supported industries are flourishing. We either have to go on as we always did, blindly join the followers of health foods, or we have to stir up our common sense and try to sort the good advice from the bad.

The sort of upheaval we are in at the moment is healthy. It is making us aware and alerting us to the importance of nutrition and the health of our families. We need not be as alarmed as some, but we should certainly not be as complacent as many of us have been. Every homemaker should remember that we are not only *what* we eat . . . we are *just as well* as we eat (we are also just as overweight as we overeat).

Natural foods and organic foods are not only the preoccupation of the young. They were the natural, uncomplicated foods many of us were raised on. Our parents had never eaten canned vegetables and fruit, and they felt that there was no excuse for using them as long as fresh foods were available. Everyone who had a few feet of ground grew vegetables on it, or people rented summer houses where there was a garden. Everything that wasn't eaten was carefully home preserved, and winters were provided for.

We lived as the epicure has always lived, on fresh fruits, on tender vegetables, on simply broiled or roasted meats eaten with their own juices. We baked bread at home and *we ate less of everything*.

The commercial production of food, the use of chemicals, are part of our enormous growth and progress. We can and should demand care, but we cannot stop the vast machinery that feeds 200 million Americans. If we followed the voices of the food faddists, we would soon have serious shortages. What each of us must do, however, is return to healthful eating—in healthful amounts. Our alarms are illogical when we do not even avail ourselves of those foods that are fresh, such as an orange.

We once had a weekend guest who asked why the orange juice tasted so strange in our house. It turned out that she (at the age of 27) had never tasted fresh orange juice before. This anecdote is interesting only because she belonged to what is described as the privileged class. Young people of every class have been victims of *shortcuts* and now they are going to the other extreme. I have spent days in health-food shops watching them read labels and select their food with seriousness and care, all of which would be even more impressive if it were more logical.

The first purpose of this book is to show that healthful eating can be epicurean. We do not necessarily have to add nutritional yeast or soybeans to our food for proper nourishment, but we do have to learn how to select the healthful foods from the vast array of food available. Those foods must then be properly prepared. The most carefully selected ingredients will do us no good if they are overcooked or if we eat too much of them.

The second purpose is to give the housewife common-sense information on how to purchase and prepare foods that will, in the present day of increased strains and lessened availability of unadulterated foods, allow her to maintain a regimen of health and well-being for her family.

The danger today is that the welcome swing back to cooking and eating for health will become just another giant fad —which is already being exploited and abused—instead of an established way of sensible living. We are in danger of jeopardizing the benefits of our new interest in healthful eating by going to extremes. Life will go on with three main meals a day and we will inevitably revert to our former eating habits and "convenience foods" unless the new way *tastes good.* The final purpose of this book is to show that there are no hardships attached to living by a healthful food regimen. Cooking wisely actually means adopting the cuisine of the epicure, who has always eaten beef in its natural juices, not under a thickened gravy, and who has always preferred a crisply broiled chicken to a smothered one.

This book is a weight-loss diet book only in the sense that a healthful food regimen is the only way to support and build good health, and health can only be fully achieved when weight is normal. Eating healthfully will reduce overweight properly. If a faster reduction is important, Chapter VII shows how to accelerate the regimen for a short period.

CHAPTER I

Preventive Eating

Most of us look upon food primarily as a source of pleasure, some of us look upon it only as a means of stopping the unpleasant sensations of hunger, but few look upon it as we should—as our source of health. Our health, and the foods we have to eat each day to maintain it, should be our prime concern, but saving time, making a living, and enjoying it have been pushed ahead of all other considerations by the present tempo of our lives.

Since our ability to work and to enjoy life depends entirely on our well-being, it is essential to place our first source of health—the food we eat—before all other concerns.

Doctor Victor Heiser, author of the best-selling biography *An American Doctor's Odyssey*, died recently at 99. It was a reassuring age to reach for the man who said, "There is nothing more important to the health of a community than proper diet. The known diseases we have left could prob-

5

ably be cut in half if we learned to eat correctly." Doctor
Heiser devoted his life to preventive measures for fighting
disease throughout the world and constantly stressed the importance of eating properly to prevent diseases.

Since we can build better health with correct nourishment
and since this health enables us, in turn, to resist and with-
stand illness, we must look upon eating as a form of preventive medicine or *preventive eating*. Actually a regimen for
the true prevention of illness would mean not only healthful
and proper food, but also the prevention of the contributing
factors of illness, overstrain, fatigue, exposure, and our constant dietary errors of overeating, undereating, crash dieting,
eating the wrong foods, and eating unhealthfully grown or
prepared foods.

The Average Body Wants to Be Well

Health is something that most of us are blessedly endowed
with. Our bodies have regenerative powers—a built-in survival kit that builds up resistance, throws off illness, and
heals itself. We are the ones who put unnecessary strains
upon our bodies. Health may be inherent in every body, but
its survival depends upon the essential foods we eat each day.
Many of us have lost sight of the support our bodies need
. . . they want to be well but we do not always cooperate.

We usually neglect healthful eating until we are no longer
entirely well or no longer as thin as we should be—which is
the same thing—and then we rely heavily and hopefully on
an abrupt change in our eating habits. We should, of course,
live on a common-sense healthy-food regimen long before
it is prescribed by a doctor.

Health is a state of body but it becomes a state of mind
when the mind does not accept its importance or overexag-
gerates it to the point of hypochondria. The wisest and most
intelligent people have been known to neglect the simplest
measures for prolonging their health. We do not seem to take

health personally; it is always something that the other man may lose.

At present we are deeply concerned with the way our foods are being grown and produced, with test-tube farming, and with its possible future effects. We should be equally concerned with our own eating habits. Half of our dietary problems can be blamed on our own mistaken selections, which in turn are often influenced by convenience and timesaving. No manufacturer would process orange juice if homemakers didn't prefer opening a can to squeezing a few fresh oranges.

Most of us eat unhealthfully to a greater or a lesser degree in spite of being the best-fed nation in the world. We make mistakes out of ignorance or laziness or lack of interest. We allow our children to start on food habits that will seriously undermine their health while we loudly condemn the occasional use of polished rice. We wouldn't have to worry about unhealthful dyes and waxes if we grew a few vegetables in the back lot, or about the preservatives used to prolong the shelf-life of a loaf of bread if we would take the time to go back to a little home baking. No one is trying to poison us. We are a nation of 200 million people and the vast system that feeds us cannot do it along the lines that sufficed a century ago. It is we who must evaluate and choose the food we eat and develop a food regimen that will support the health of our families.

Common-sense healthful eating is not a matter of looking for substitutes for the foods now generally considered nonhealthful. If we believe that granulated sugar is not good for our children, then this is the time to cut down on the amount of sugar they eat rather than substituting honey or molasses for it. There is no point whatever in breading a croquette with whole-wheat crumbs when the deep-fat frying is infinitely worse for us than the few white breadcrumbs could ever be. We need a change from the unhealthful preparations and amounts we have been eating—not substitutions that will enable us to continue the same mistakes we have been making all along.

Honey and brown sugar do taste good, and there is every

reason for using them in desserts for growing children, for the elderly, and for guests, but the only way to avoid the consequences of constant overindulgence in sweets is to *avoid* them. There is enough natural sugar in fruits, which we should eat, and in an occasional dessert sweetened with honey or brown sugar to take care of our nutritional requirements.

Eating healthfully does not mean an unpleasant diet as many of us seem to think. The good things in life are not necessarily the harmful ones, although a great many of them are, and pleasures need not be sacrificed in order to be well. The program for healthful eating may look a little like a reducing diet, but the way most people are eating today looks exactly like a *gaining diet*—and apparently that is what it ultimately achieves.

Eating to Protect Natural Health

The basic rules for healthful eating divide into four groups:

1. When and how to eat
2. What cooking processes to use
3. What foods to eat in what rotation
4. How to eat away from home

Eating healthfully will ultimately adjust your weight to the correct level, but if you have a weight problem turn to Chapter VII for a healthy weight-loss regimen. Then come back to healthful eating after the weight has been lost.

When and How to Eat

1. *Eat three times a day* and not between meals.

2. *Eat only when hungry.* The old French proverb that the appetite comes while eating is a fallacy. The appetite must be there *before* eating, and eating should stop when it is appeased. Rules 1 and 2 appear to contradict each

other, but they actually depend on each other. When we eat three times a day (without exception) we will be naturally and normally hungry three times a day. *Eat only when hungry* must also be applied during the meal—stop eating as soon as the sense of hunger has disappeared.

3. *Take small helpings* to begin with so that you will not be influenced by a sense of obligation to finish what is on your plate.

4. *Eat slowly and chew well.* This does not mean dawdling over food but it does mean that it should ·not be slung down without proper chewing.

5. *Do not wash down foods with liquids.* Drink when you are thirsty between meals but avoid drinking liquids with meals. It leads to overeating.

6. *Never eat or drink extremely hot or extremely cold foods or beverages.* Let hot beverages cool off slightly and let ice cream melt in your mouth before swallowing it. Eat food only after it stops sizzling.

7. *Never eat when you are tired, nervous, emotionally upset, or in a great hurry.* It is better to skip a meal than to combine it with pressures, unpleasantness, or fatigue.

What Cooking Processes to Use

1. Eat foods that are:

Baked	Lightly sautéed
Boiled	Pan fried
Braised	Roasted
Broiled	Rotisseried
Grilled	Steamed

2. Do not eat deep-fat or shallow-fat-fried foods, batter-fried or breaded and fried foods. Do not dredge foods in flour and then fry them in fat.

3. Eat more raw and uncooked foods.

What Foods to Eat in What Rotation

1. First and most important, eat a great variety of foods. No *single-food* diet should be followed. The only way to insure an adequate intake of essential nutrients is to eat a wide variety of foods.

2. Eat everything—dairy products, eggs, fish, meat, poultry, vegetables, and fruit—but eat in different rotations and in different proportions.

3. Make fruits and vegetables half of your daily food intake and eat half of the fruits and vegetables uncooked.

4. Start each meal with fruit or a fruit salad and go on to raw or uncooked vegetables; only then eat meat and end with cheese, nuts, or unsulphured dried fruits instead of dessert. Serve desserts only to children, the elderly, and guests. The sugar in the fruit will satisfy your craving for desserts, so do not eat desserts out of habit.

5. Always eat whole fruits or vegetables in preference to juices. The interaction of the whole fruit or vegetable and your digestion is more beneficial to your system as well as doing more to satisfy hunger. Liquids pass through with less benefit.

6. Do not eat flour-thickened gravies, sauces, or soups. The combination of flour and fat, like desserts, should be limited to times when you eat out.

7. Eat natural foods, not in the sense of the present search for "natural foods," but in the sense of fresh fruit being more natural than frozen or canned fruit, sprouted-wheat or whole-grain bread more natural than a croissant. A piece of broiled or roasted meat served with only its own juices is more natural than a breadcrumbed chop fried in shallow fat. *You can recognize these natural foods by the fact that they are less complicated, less has been done to them, less has been taken away from them or returned to them.*

8. When rule 7 is properly applied the menu will automatically be based on the healthiest foods prepared in the healthiest way. There will be no canned foods, no bleached flour, no refined sugars, and no high seasonings. If fresh fruits and vegetables are unavailable, then substitute dried vegetables or frozen if necessary. Quick-frozen fish should be eaten in preference to canned fish.

9. Soups should only be eaten *instead* of, not *in addition to*, another course.

How to Eat Away From Home

When you are eating at restaurants, traveling, or dining at the homes of friends the healthful eating regimen can be skipped—no food regimen should ever be imposed upon others unless it is essential to your health. If, however, you spend long periods away from home or have to eat lunch at work, then the health regimen should be followed as much as possible.

At restaurants, order a fresh fruit, not juice, at the beginning of the meal, and a salad to follow the fruit. The egg dishes often include eggs in combination with vegetables, which are always desirable if they are not bound with a cream sauce. Hollandaise sauce is another way to eat egg with vegetables.

If a main course is desired, look at the fish first and select one that is broiled. Select only meat or poultry that is grilled, broiled, or roasted. Skip the desserts in favor of cheese.

Working luncheons can always consist of fruit, a healthy sandwich, or salad.

CHAPTER II

Fads, Facts, and Natural Foods

The importance of preserving our natural health by eating properly has been written about and preached through the centuries. Interest in the subject has come and gone, and health movements are nothing new. The United States has supported several major health crusaders, such as John Harvey Kellogg of Battle Creek, Michigan, who first advocated the general use of cereal flakes on every American breakfast table. He also encouraged everyone to eat slowly and chew well. Battle Creek Sanatorium became a major health resort. *Postum* and *Corn Flakes* were part of C. W. Post's health promotion program and became the basis of a vast fortune. Bernarr MacFadden turned his interest in health into a publishing fortune; he was a pioneer in popularizing enriched flour, sunbathing, and fitness, and published *Physical Culture*, later called *Health Review*. But while millions have followed, other millions have blissfully sustained, supported, and assisted the food industry in producing "better and better" and easier-to-prepare foods.

At the moment we are involved in a major health-food upheaval composed of reason, nonsense, and about two billion dollars a year. It cannot be ignored but it has to be sorted out with common sense. The warnings on which this thriving industry is based are often overexaggerated, but the fact remains that public interest has been aroused, and those responsible for the protection of our food and health are increasing their efforts. The health-food movement, whether we support it or not, is to our benefit.

Most people have reacted either by ignoring the warnings that are being sounded or by going to great lengths to find replacements and substitutions for what we are now told are the errors in our eating ways. Very few of us have arrived at the simplest and proper answer . . . to do without or, at least, to cut down. If we truly believe that refined sugar does us harm, then we should indeed substitute honey or brown or raw sugars—but most important of all, we should cut down on sugar altogether.

Some of the foods that are now most strenuously avoided are the inevitable outcome of our country's growth. But we are also protesting and worrying about a situation we have brought upon ourselves by our largely snobbish demands. We have insisted on the rich man's white bread, the most-bleached flours and the most-refined sugars. Not only are we to blame for creating the demand, we are the ones who have over-indulged ourselves. Producers have only give us what we wanted and what constitutes "consumer tastes."

Some of us are now virtually trying to turn the clock back to a time when our great grandparents were eating healthfully grown foods, butter made from unpasteurized cream, less glossy green vegetables, and much less pretty fruit. (To which we must add that our great grandparents didn't sling down their luncheons in ten minutes, rush about as we do, or try to take constant shortcuts in the kitchen.)

We cannot recapture the past. We may seek out organically grown foods, but we have all seen what wind can do to spread dust or chemicals over wide areas. We cannot control what water is used or what pesticides are sprayed on adjacent trees. Those of us who have never eaten canned foods are not affected by the supposed dangers of their processing. But we are all proud of the superior growth and quality of our meats and the broader white breasts of our birds (the most-sought-after delicacy in Europe is an imported frozen American turkey). All this magic is accomplished with good feeding and some drugs, and most Americans would not want to return to a scrawny bird. Few foods have not been somehow treated by chemicals that make them grow better or free them from pests.

Even if a family today were to prepare only organically grown foods, they would have to eat all their meals at home, or in health-food restaurants (no substitute for the full lobster dinner at the Old Stage Coach), or with equally interested and conscientious friends, in order to maintain a nonchemical diet. Working people who are away from home in the middle of the day *may* be employed by companies which have put in a health-food luncheon, but it is doubtful. The best answer is to approach the entire subject sensibly and to start once and for all on a healthful regimen that will eliminate many of the threats. A large part of our daily food is not healthful whether it is prepared from beneficial or unbeneficial ingredients.

When I was a child I read a book that had an alarming illustration of a man chained to a tree, reading a large book. The message was simple—he had been perfectly happy until he learned to read; then he discovered that the world was round and he was terrified of falling off. We too were, and should remain, perfectly happy with our magnificent food, but now we are beginning to read and make discoveries that we do not understand. Many of us are alarmed . . . but we cannot chain ourselves to a tree. At this point there are only two things we can do within reason: *avoid* and *prevent*.

Avoidance can only be accomplished in part. We cannot stop eating market foods and we cannot possibly raise all our own food, but we can avoid certain foods, which were not good for us at any time. We can avail ourselves of the organic foods that are raised and processed without chemicals and additives, if we are convinced of their benefits. Organic-food shops are springing up all over the country, and some farmers are going back to growing their produce without chemicals, although many are still reluctant.

Prevention means building up our own resistance, increasing our general health and strength—and that of our children—so that we can resist weakening illnesses as well as the harm that may lie in foods that have been bleached, refined, or treated with agricultural chemicals. What cannot be stressed too much is that this *resistance* to unhealthful foods is the same resistance to illness that everyone should build up throughout their lives by a program of natural, healthful eating for a full and healthy life.

The doctor who tells his patient that a mild attack is *a blessing in disguise, because it serves as a warning,* is doing what we hope the awareness of our situation is doing for us— warning us, not just to stop eating certain polished foods, but to stop eating unhealthfully. A very primitive example is the young woman who gives up Danish pastry or a doughnut on her coffee break because they contain bleached flour and refined sugar, which she has learned may be detrimental to her health. If she is going to forgo the coffee break it should be for more valid reasons than the possible harm of sugar and flour. She should give it up because: 1. Eating between meals may not harm her when she is young and thin, but it will be a difficult habit to break when she is beginning to put on weight when she is older. 2. Coffee is not a health beverage. 3. The sugar in the coffee and in the pastry *may* give her energy but an orange would do the same without laying the foundation for overweight. 4. Pastries and cakes have never been on any really healthful regimen. Aside from the positive, long-range (about twenty years) threat of obesity, a deep-fat-fried doughnut is by no means the most easily digestible thing to eat with hot coffee in the middle of the morning.

If she gives up the unhealthful habit because of the minimal threat of the flour in the pastry (and then eats creamed turkey on white-bread toast and a piece of layer cake for lunch) her reason for giving up the coffee break is defeated— but any reason is good enough if it breaks her of a habit that is unhealthful on three or four more serious counts. If, because of early rising and the ardors of reaching the office (and the temptation of *seeing* and *smelling* the coffee cart) she has to eat before noon, then an orange or an apple or a thin slice of buttered full-kernel bread with a cup of tea would be much more beneficial. Tea need not be black or green. Tea bags of camomile or rose hip tea can be taken to the office, as can fruit or a thin sandwich. Drinking tea without a sweetener can be learned in about a week of gritting your teeth . . . after that sweet tea tastes hideous.

Buying Natural Foods

We have no control whatever over food eaten away from home, luncheons eaten during working hours, or meals eaten when visiting or traveling, but we can control what we serve at home to some extent. The average American is home for at least 1½ meals a day. We *could* therefore eat wisely for at least half of the time, which is half the battle won. We are up against two separate problems simultaneously: a general program of unwise, unhealthful eating, brought about by the haste and tensions of our times, and the possible threat of certain foods that (also as a result of our progressive times) are no longer grown and processed naturally. We are confronted with the problem of selecting a common-sense middle course that will not upset the budget, will satisfy our long-established taste preferences, and will still protect our health. We must make the decision, once and for all, to think of a long term of health for ourselves and our families, as against the ease of opening a can or a package.

If the decision is made to shift to organically grown natural foods, it will cause an upheaval in our marketing routines, as well as in our budget and menu-making. If we are going to have an upheaval anyway, we might as well shift to a more healthful eating regimen at the same time. If we have gained new awareness of the possible latent dangers that lie in our daily fare, then we should also realize that the purest, most healthfully grown, and least processed foods will do us no good if we eat the wrong ones, or if we boil everything out of them, or if we wolf them down without chewing— just when we are tired, worried, emotionally upset, and not hungry anyway.

The new program may mean going to an organic-food store, as well as a health-food department in the supermarket. It may mean the trouble of mail-ordering some product or driving to a distant mill for stone-ground flours. In some homes it will mean baking your own bread, and in most cases it will mean the trouble of shelling peas or slicing beans and doing all the food preparations we had forgotten. All of it will cost more in time; a working person would not be able to prepare a healthful meal in an hour. If organically grown vegetables are used their cost will be higher than those from the market due to limited production.

Many Americans are sorting out a common-sense middle way between the extremes of today's fads and exaggeration and the complete disinterest of the past. They are finding that they can eat as well as, indeed better than, they ever did before, by selecting foods that are not canned or frozen or factory processed. They are learning to read labels and evaluate, and they are watching the packaging materials. All of it will probably cost about 25 percent more than you have been setting aside for marketing in the past.

There is at present a close relationship between the purchasing of healthy foods (and health foods) and the paycheck, or the economic status of the family. The families whose incomes are low consume about two-thirds as much meat, poultry and eggs as the better-situated families, but they consume more bread. They buy half as many vegetables and much less than half as much fresh fruit. Going in for healthful eating should not mean, and probably cannot mean, an increase in spending, so it is only possible with a shift in the budget.

There has to be a saving somewhere to allow for new expenses.

I have seen carts come through the checkout counter of the supermarket loaded with packaged luncheon meats, ready-baked cakes and pies, canned vegetables, fruits, and fruit juices, sliced porous white bread, and boxes of crackers and snacks—not a green leaf or fresh fruit in sight. This cartful of treasures costs the same as lots of fruits and vegetables, meat, bacon, butter, oil, and full-kernel bread.

There is no question that the shift to healthy foods and natural foods means more preparation. With fresh or organically grown vegetables, we have to do the work that the canneries and frozen-food suppliers have been doing for us. We can no longer pop things into a little boiling water or heat partially prepared foods. We cannot open a can or a package and prepare dinner in minutes. Eating healthfully and going back to nature means going back to scraping carrots, cleaning celery, peeling and preparing—and on top of that the food costs more. If it is all to work on the old budget there have to be radical rearrangements.

One might suppose we could economize by eliminating all the factory-prepared foods, which are made more expensive by the very processes that do us no good. Why pay to have your rice polished and your sugar refined when you are not buying yourself additional health value for your money? But it doesn't work that way. The loaf of white bread produced in enormous quantities is bound to be cheaper than the small-quantity production of full-kernel breads. The healthy loaf of home-baked whole-kernel bread becomes stale and deteriorates faster, and the loss is consequently greater. In many areas freshly grown or organically grown foods and health foods have to be brought from great distances or imported. Their cost is naturally higher.

With all these changes in our routine, there is no point in half measures. Do not spend more money on organically grown foods and bake your own whole-wheat bread on one hand and then fit into the same old menu mistakes on the other.

What Are Natural Foods?

Natural foods are unaided by chemicals. They do not depend on the test tube to protect them from pestilence, to increase their growth, to keep them from deteriorating, or to make them visually more appealing.

They break down into three groups.

1. *Organically grown fruits and vegetables:* These fruits, berries, and vegetables are grown in rich, natural soil, without the use of insecticides, herbicides, or chemicals. The soil is enriched and conditioned with manure or its equivalent, humus and compost, and it has been so treated for a specified number of years. The water used in the growing of organic foods has to be pure and unpolluted.

2. *Natural food:* This refers to organically grown food after it has ripened and been picked. It is unprocessed, not treated with preservatives, artificial bleaches, colors, or waxes. As a result of being *organically grown* and *naturally presented* the fruits and vegetables are usually smaller and less eye-appealing than treated produce. Because they are grown and distributed in smaller quantities and because they are more perishable, they are also more expensive. While we do not know to what extent the fruits and vegetables that are grown nonorganically are injurious to health, we all know or remember how good freshly picked home-grown garden vegetables used to be. They are tender and delicious, and anyone who has land and the time to tend a garden should certainly grow his own organic and natural foods.

It should, however, always be remembered that if all our produce were suddenly grown without fertilizers and were shipped to market without preservatives, our crops and our supplies could diminish by more than one half.

It should also be remembered that the rate and amount of processing increases as the life of the product is extended. A freshly grown, organic, natural food is ideal, but a fresh fruit or vegetable that is grown with chemical fertilizers and processed and parched to remain fresh for a short time is still more desirable than foods that have been further processed by freezing and by canning.

Finally we must remember that we are dependent on the integrity of the organic-food farmer, the distributor, and the shop from which we buy, just as we are dependent on the integrity of the large-scale farmers who supply the supermarkets. We rely upon the organic-food farmer not to use any insecticides, chemical fertilizers, or polluted water, and we depend on the large-scale farmer to use them in moderation. It would be virtually impossible to institute the daily checks and tests that would be necessary to prove conclusively that all food sold as *organically* grown and *naturally* presented is actually just that. The shop from which you buy is dependent on distributors, who are dependent on their suppliers. The farmer may be checked at intervals, but he is not controlled each day. The small garden or a sort of garden-pool, run by a conscientious group, is the most dependable way of obtaining organic natural food. It is also the way great-grandmother— whom we are trying to emulate—got the vegetables and fruits she served her family in season and preserved for her family for the out-of-season months.

3. *Naturally fed meats and free-range eggs:* Naturally fed or organically raised meat and poultry comes from livestock raised on natural pasturage and on fodder that has been organically grown without use of chemicals, as described above. Naturally fed animals and birds are not given additional antibiotics, hormones, or chemicals to improve their appetites, growth, or the quality of their meat. Free-range eggs come from hens that are allowed to range across natural land on which neither fertilizers nor insecticides have been used. The additional feed that they are given is organically raised and not treated with chemicals.

Whole-Grain Flours and Meals

These are obtained by grinding the entire kernel of the grain into flour, which means that nothing beneficial is lost in the milling process. Stone-ground whole-grain flours are considered the most desirable because the stone-grinding process does not generate as high a temperature as the steel rollers do and enzymes are not destroyed.

It should, however, be remembered that when this flour is used in baking bread or cakes the oven temperatures are higher than the destructive temperatures of the steel rollers that mill the flour, so some enzymes are destroyed in the natural baking process.

The whole-wheat, rye, oat, millet, buckwheat, and corn flours are all available now, as is vacuum-packed wheat germ. With the exception of the wheat germ, they are all perishable and should be bought fresh in small quantities and stored in the refrigerator. These grains vary, and the recipes on the packages are usually the best to use in baking with that particular flour.

Although some nutrients are unavoidably lost when white flour is milled, it is later re-enriched to the natural level of the original product. Because of the recent interest in the whole-grain breads and cereals, some loaves of sprouted-wheat and whole-wheat breads are now widely available in all parts of the country at the regular markets. The stone-ground whole-grain flours are also appearing on all market shelves and need no longer be purchased at health-food stores. See the Mail Order List at the back of the book.

Honey

Honey is a sweet liquid prepared by bees from nectars they collect from plants and store for food. It is flavored by the flowers or plants from which the bees gather the nectar, and it may be named or classified according to the flower source that is the chief source of the honey. When there are two prominent sources the honey may be labeled by the double name, as Orange-Grapefruit Honey. *The choice of honey flavor is entirely a matter of taste. One is not more or less beneficial than the others.*

Honey is also classified by the method of production or presentation to the market. *Extracted honey* (strained honey) is honey which has been separated from the comb. *Liquid honey* is free of visible crystals. *Crystallized honey* (candied, granulated, or "spread") is solidified honey, which may be natural or produced. *Comb honey* in various forms is honey contained in the same cells of the wax comb in which it was produced. The color of the various honeys is not a quality factor, but an optical property.

The best processing of honey as presented in the market is the minimum processing. Raw honey will ferment, and honeys that are processed to remain liquid and not to ferment, for better appearance, inevitably lose flavor and possibly some of their quality. Honeys are at their best in the comb. If an extracted honey is preferred, however, a granulated honey is recommended, because the heat that is used to prevent granulation and fermentation causes a deterioration in quality.

Honey is the only predigested nature product and, being readily assimilated, it is a quick source of energy. It is primarily a carbohydrate food. Carbohydrates are not definitely needed for nutrition but they provide most of the energy we need to live. Before the body uses most carbohydrates (with the exception of the monosaccharides) it must digest them into their simple sugar components. But the monosaccharides —dextrose, glucose, levulose (or fructose), and others—are absorbed directly into the blood stream from the intestine. The sugars in honey are monosaccharides: levulose (fruit sugar), dextrose (grape sugar), sucrose (table sugar), and others. The sugars in honey are thus ready for assimilation on reaching the intestine and save the body the step of hydrolyzing, or digesting. In other words, the bees take over one step and present us with a product that is more easily digested and energizes more rapidly than other carbohydrates, and tastes good too.

Calories and carbohydrates in honey. One tablespoon of honey contains approximately 64 calories and 17.3 grams carbohydrate. Granulated sugar contains approximately 47 calories per tablespoon and 12.1 grams of carbohydrates. Brown sugar contains 49 calories and 12.8 grams of carbohydrates per tablespoon. Sifted confectioners' sugar contains 23 calories and 5.9 grams carbohydrate per tablespoon. One tablespoon molasses contains from 43 to 57 calories, depending on its quality and from 11.0 to 15.0 grams carbohydrate.

Besides being an important factor in the feeding of infants and children, honey has been a beneficial source of energy to everyone who does strenuous work or who participates in sports. It is used by wrestlers, track athletes, swimmers, marathon runners, bicycle racers, and mountain climbers (Sir Edmund P. Hillary used honey in his conquest of Mount Everest in May of 1953).

The honey years. Honey is of value during three ages: in the nutrition of infants and children, as a source of energy during the athletic years, and for the elderly.

Remember that honey should only be used by diabetics under a physician's direction.

Cooking with honey. Honey adds flavor to foods and increases keeping qualities. In baking, it has the added advantage of making the products moist and palatable for long periods. Honey cookies may seem dry when they come out of the oven, but they soften in a short time and will not dry out again if properly stored. They remain fresh for months, which probably explains why so many Christmas breads and cookies are still the traditional honey cakes that can be baked long before Christmas. Honey absorbs moisture, which adds to its advantages when it is used in baking breads. But keep in mind that high cooking and baking temperatures are destructive to honey's flavor and color. Honey should never be allowed to reach the boiling point because valuable enzymes are destroyed.

Honey may be substituted for sugar as a sweetening agent

where small quantities of sugar are used—for example, in tea or iced tea, lemonade, fruit cake, salad dressings, and in baking bread or muffins. Where small amounts of sugar are concerned honey may be substituted measure for measure. In baking cakes or cookies that call for a large amount of sugar, honey may still be substituted but the amount of liquid in the recipe has to be adjusted. *Where large amounts of sugar are concerned, honey may be substituted measure for measure, but for each cup of honey reduce the liquid called for in the recipe by ¼ cup, or 4 tablespoons.* For example, if a cake recipe calls for adding ½ cup shortening, 1 cup sugar and ¾ cup sour milk or buttermilk to the usual flour and eggs, it can be changed as follows: Cream ½ cup shortening with 1 cup honey until almost white, then add flour and ½ cup sour milk or buttermilk in the usual way. These facts should be remembered in using your own recipes or in cooking out of any cookbook. *Also remember that in baking any recipe containing honey, the oven temperatures should not exceed 350° to 375° F. or "moderate."*

Substitutions, however, are rarely wholly successful and the healthiest way to eat honey is as a sweetener in beverages or as a spread. Here again it would be better to omit cakes and other sweet baked goods from the diet than to make substitutions. A piece of cake on a birthday or other festive occasion will taste much better and do less harm (where weight is concerned) than weekly cakes made of whole-wheat flour and honey.

History of honey. The use of honey goes back to prehistoric man. It was our only sweetening agent until sugar was produced commercially. The first knowledge of sugar cane came with the campaigns of Alexander the Great in 327 B.C., but the original use of cane sugar did not go beyond chewing it until about 300 A.D., when it was used for healing in India. Sugar was not in use in Europe until after the first refinery was opened in Augsburg in 1573, and it was only in the seventeenth and eighteenth centuries that it began to take the place of honey among the wealthy. With the discovery of beet sugar and the building of the first factory for its production in Germany in 1801, sugar gradually replaced honey. In recent years honey is again being substituted for sugar to a limited extent.

Storing honey. Deterioration can be avoided by storing honey at temperatures under 50° F. Storage temperatures of 80° F. and over, even for short periods, *must* be avoided.

Fats and Oils

Fats are found in butter and margarine, oils and shortenings, and in lesser degrees in cream, nuts, cheeses, and meats. The low-fat foods are lean meats, most fish, nonfat milk, shellfish, fruits, and vegetables. Both animals and plants make fats; the animal fats are usually hard, while the vegetables fats are more apt to be liquid, such as oil. The hard fats are called *saturated* fats and the oils, or plant fats, are called *unsaturated* or *polyunsaturated* fats. Different fats have shifted in popularity and use. Twenty years ago about twice as much butter as margarine was used as a spread for bread at the table. Now the figures are reversed. Vegetable oils or margarine are used more in cooking and the vegetable oils are now popular as salad oils. Lard is not used as much in cooking or baking but is now an important ingredient in solid shortenings and similar products.

The calorie content of fats and oils is as follows:

1 tablespoon salad oil, vegetable oil, or olive oil	125 calories
1 tablespoon lard	125 calories
1 tablespoon chicken fat	125 calories
1 tablespoon vegetable shortening	110 calories
1 tablespoon butter	100 to 102 calories
1 tablespoon margarine	100 to 109 calories
1 tablespoon whipped margarine	70 calories
1 tablespoon whipped butter	68 calories
1 tablespoon imitation margarine	50 calories

Margarine is fortified with vitamin A, while butter contains it naturally. The aeration process used in whipped margarine and butter increases the volume and consequently reduces the number of calories by about one-third less than the number found in an equal amount of plain butter or margarine. The new imitation margarines contain about 40 percent butter and other fats instead of the 80 percent contained in regular margarine.

Butter is USDA rated and must contain 80 percent milk fat. The only permitted additions are salt and coloring substances. *Margarine,* or *oleomargarine,* was developed in France about one hundred years ago as a butter substitute. It has become increasingly popular in recent years since an *imitation margarine,* which contains about half as many calories per tablespoon as regular margarine or butter, has been put on the market. Both butter and margarine absorb the flavor of other food and should be stored in a separate compartment in the refrigerator. For information on butter made from raw certified cream, see page 27.

The housewife is often confused by the many edible oils and fats. There is no reason for buying any of these products in a health-food store at inflated prices. All well-supplied markets carry a full line of oils and fats including USDA butters with the highest AA rating.

A healthful eating program should contain animal and vegetable fats each day—in moderation. The two most desirable fats for this purpose are butter and a pure vegetable oil, preferably olive oil. Because olive oil is expensive and has a distinctive taste, a combination of three parts pure vegetable oil—corn oil, sunflower, peanut, or safflower oil—to one part olive oil makes an ideal basis for dressings and mayonnaises. Salads and raw vegetables play such an important part in healthful meal planning that salad dressings and mayonnaises are the logical vehicles for the necessary daily supply of oil.

As a health regimen is demonstrably a weight-controlling diet, there is no danger that moderate amounts of these fats will increase weight. If, for purposes of encouragement, a faster weight loss is desired, the fats and oils can be cut down to the minimum for about two weeks.

Dairy Products

Very few people go through a day without consuming one or more of the basic dairy products—milk, cream, ice cream, butter, and cheese. Children need fresh milk during the growing years, but adults usually get their required daily amounts of dairy foods from other milk products. (Ice cream, while not a recommended health food, is listed here so that it is not eaten as a *supplement* to other dairy products.)

A true health regimen for an adult does not include white sauces, but it must include about 1 tablespoon of fat or oil each day.

Buy your milk, cream, and butter at the supermarket. Some of the health-food stores offer better cream cheeses, cottage cheeses, and yogurt than the supermarket, but the best cheeses can usually be found in the cheese specialty shops that exist in many areas today. Some supermarkets also offer a wide selection of domestic and imported cheeses, and some cheeses can be mail ordered.

Raw certified milk. Doctors and nutritional experts agree that the advantages of raw certified milk are far outweighed by the safety of pasteurized milk. Some people, however, believe that if raw certified cream is obtainable, the housewife should put it into her electric beater to make small quantities of butter, which should be set aside for table purposes. Raw milk and cream contain amino acids, enzymes, and other nutrients that are destroyed in pasteurization. Pasteurization, on the other hand, destroys harmful bacteria. The few dairies that sell raw certified milk, from specially fed and supervised cows, have to be tested periodically and licensed to sell their products. Health-food stores usually carry raw certified milk.

The most commonly used dairy products are:

Whole milk. Cream rises to top of bottle or container
Homogenized milk. The fat (or cream) is distributed through the milk
Skimmed milk. Most fat is removed, as are vitamins A and D. Vitamins A and D are added in fortified skim milk (also in nonfat and lowfat milk)
Flavored milk. Whole milk with chocolate and sweetener added
Cultured milk. Bacterial cultures are added to milk
Buttermilk. Usually made from skimmed milk
Yogurt. Semisolid, frequently flavored with fruit, vanilla, or coffee
Canned milk. Water is removed and milk is concentrated
Evaporated milk. Sterilized with vitamin D added
Condensed milk. Sugar added as a preservative
Dry milk (whole, nonfat or dry skim milk). Made from whole milk or fluid skim milk
Half-and-half. Mixture of milk and cream or milk and sour cream
Cream (light, heavy, and sour). Contains at least 18 percent milk fat and is usually homogenized
Ice cream. Hard or soft frozen dessert made from cream, milk, sugar, flavorings, and stabilizers
Ice milk. Made from milk instead of cream
Frozen custard. Made as ice cream with the addition of egg yolks
Sherbet. Made from milk, fruit juices, sweeteners, and stabilizers
Cheese. There are more than four hundred varieties of natural cheeses as well as pasteurized process and cold-pack or club cheeses

Condiments, Spices, Herbs, and Flavorings

While herbs do not cure everything that ails you, as herbalists and enthusiasts claim, they add fragrance and flavor to food. Many of them do have healthful properties. They can add a savory touch to recipes when a dieter is breaking the habit of oversalting all food.

The same cannot be said for the condiments and spices. Taken in small amounts they are not harmful, but continued use of highly spiced and seasoned foods, hot peppers, and sharp sauces in our climate is definitely not a healthful food regimen. After long periods of oversalting and overspicing all foods, it is hard to break the salt-cellar habit. Unseasoned foods taste bland and uninteresting, and it takes several weeks before the more subtle and less obtrusive fresh flavors of food can be tasted and appreciated.

The *seasonings* and flavorings that can be used instead of salt are varied and surprisingly effective. Lemon juice, a pinch of brown sugar, saffron, black, white, or red pepper (in moderation), paprika, orange peel, cider vinegar, and all the herbs add zest and interest.

Salt is composed of two elements, sodium and chlorine. Great natural quantities of sodium chloride—or common salt—are found in rock salt and solar salt (which is produced by the action of the sun on sea water). Sodium is an essential mineral nutrient of which we require about .5 to 1.0 gram per day, or about $\frac{1}{4}$ teaspoon. All the salt we require is probably found in the foods we eat, but we use a great deal more. Salt helps to retain water in the body and for that reason should be reduced where weight is being watched. There are also medical reasons for cutting down on salt, in which case herbs and some spices make excellent substitutes.

The salt we add to our food before, during, or after cooking is not the only sodium we consume. A low-salt diet is very different from a sodium-restricted diet, and while using less salt or no salt is advisable for healthful eating, a sodium-restricted diet must be done under the guidance of a physician.

Sea salt is produced in small quantities by natural evaporation of uncontaminated sea water. Pharmacies, health-food stores, and specialty-food shops carry it in crystallized form, which can be ground through a wooden salt mill. Imported natural sea salt, Sel de Mer from France and Maldon Table

Sea Salt from England are excellent. To order them, see the Mail Order List on page 248.

The function of salt in the body with regard to water retention and dieting is explained in Chapter VII.

Flavorings such as pure vanilla or lemon and orange rind enhance various dishes and are desirable for that reason. Artificial flavorings should be avoided, not because all of them are harmful, but because the fresh, pure flavor is always to be preferred over the artificial.

Alcoholic Beverages

Most adults in the United States drink alcoholic beverages although it has long been established that most are unhealthful in less or greater degrees depending on the individual and on the quantity consumed. Some beverages, such as beer and light ales, are considered healthful because they are nourishing, and the often-recommended glass of port wine or sherry for the elderly is considered a slight stimulant and tonic. We are not concerned with the fact of drinking, but rather with the facts that should be remembered about it. Alcohol is usually a stimulant that provides an average of 150 calories per cocktail or highball, more if the cocktail is very sweet. Someone who drinks two or three cocktails before dinner, wine with the meal, and a whisky and soda after, is accounting for anywhere from one fourth to one half of his daily calorie limit without the slightest benefit. Because there are no vitamins, minerals, or necessary proteins in cocktails and because they are usually taken very cold on an empty stomach, they cannot be listed here as health beverages. If weight is being watched, a cocktail should be taken instead of an unessential part of the daily diet, but never instead of the essential meats, vegetables, and fruits. Give up desserts and snacks for every cocktail and watch your weight.

How to Use Your Cookbooks and Recipe File

Cooking according to a healthful food regimen does not require a series of cookbooks. It depends, instead, on a series of rules that should be applied to all cookbooks.

1. If a recipe calls for sugar, you can safely reduce its amount and substitute either dark, light brown, or raw sugar, on a spoonful-for-spoonful basis. To substitute honey for sugar, see pages 23–24.

2. Wherever a small quantity of salt is called for, leave it out completely. Where a large quantity is required, learn to reduce it, little by little, until you are using less than half as much as you did. Remember that the normal daily requirement of salt is only ¼ teaspoon.

3. In almost all cases where food is to be boiled, reduce the amount of water and steam it instead.

4. Wherever cooking times can be slightly reduced, do so. We may have learned to broil food correctly, but on the whole we overcook our food.

5. Watch quantities and cook only the amounts recommended in Chapter IV. Most cookbooks recommend larger amounts than are necessary, which leads to overeating or too many leftovers.

6. Scrub potatoes and boil them in their jackets. Either eat them skin and all or, if the recipe calls for peeled potatoes, draw off the skins after the potatoes are boiled.

7. If the recipe specifies shortcuts with canned or frozen products, substitute fresh foods wherever possible. Use fresh foods and replace them with frozen foods only when fresh ones are not available. Try not to use canned vegetables when fresh or frozen can be used in their stead. Do not use recipes with canned meats or luncheon meats.

8. Where recipes call for fried foods, either skip the recipe or broil or pan-broil the food.

9. Use low-fat diet margarine, butter, or sunflower, safflower, corn, or similar oils in cooking. Do not use lard or animal fats.

10. All recipes using white bread, white breadcrumbs, or white bread in any form should be changed to whole-wheat or whole-grain bread or breadcrumbs, or bread should be omitted entirely.

11. Substitute brown or unpolished rice for all recipes that call for rice. Wild rice may also be substituted, but not when rice is combined with any sweetener.

12. Do not prepare recipes dependent on white flour or pasta. Make whole-wheat noodles to substitute for egg noodles.

13. Leave out pie crusts, cakes, and cookies completely or learn to make an unsweetened pie crust out of whole-wheat flour. Graham cracker and similar crusts sweetened with brown sugar are also permissible, but fruit or cheese make more healthful desserts.

14. Skip every recipe that combines flour and butter or fat—in other words, white sauce or brown sauce. Do not make gravies. Learn to enjoy meat with its natural juices (do not overcook the meat to begin with) and make Hollandaise or egg sauces to substitute for flour-thickened sauces. Remember to count the eggs, oil, or butter in these sauces as part of your weekly ration.

15. Wherever a recipe calls for *dredging with flour,* turn to something else. Use whole-grain flours where necessary, but do not brown flour in fat or oil.

16. Use homemade stock where stocks are called for. Canned consommé and bouillon contain a great deal of salt.

17. Omit flour-thickened soups and go lightly on substituting cream.

18. Bake whole-grain breads instead of white breads. See the rules for substituting whole-grain flours for white flour in your regular recipes, page 202.

19. In salad-making substitute cider vinegar or homemade vinegar for wine vinegar, fresh herbs for dried, freshly chopped onion for onion flakes. Use fresh greens. A healthful salad should not be a place for leftovers or shortcuts.

20. Save the water in which well-scrubbed potatoes or vegetables were cooked. Use potato water in baking and vegetable broth for sauces or vegetable stocks.

Glossary of Newly Used Terms

Acids.   See Amino Acids.

Additives.   Substances obtained from natural or manufactured sources, added to improve the nutritive value of food or enhance its flavor or color. Also added to food as a preservative or to retard spoilage.

Amino acids.   The group of 22 amino acids forms the basis from which proteins are constructed. Of these, 14 are manufactured by the body. The remaining 8 are called the essential amino acids and can only be obtained from food. Good sources are milk, milk products, eggs, fish, poultry, and liver.

Bacillus bulgaris.   Also called lactobacillus bulgaricus. A bacteria added to milk to produce the cultured-milk product known as yogurt.

Balanced diet.   The combination of essential nutrients required per day for a healthful food regimen. Needs differ with age and activity. A balanced diet obviates the use of supplements. It should contain foods from the milk, meat, fruit, and vegetable groups as well as from the starch or bread and cereal group.

Binders.   Agents or vehicles used in foods to cause a mixture to cohere.

Bleaches.   Agents used to whiten or withdraw color from food, as celery. Bread flours may be bleached or unbleached. Pastry flour is usually unbleached while cake flour is always bleached.

Brewers' yeast.   Not to be confused with bakers' yeast, it is rich in minerals and vitamins and is an excellent source for protein. Often prescribed in weight-loss diets because it contains few calories but satisfies the feeling of hunger.

Calorie.   A unit used to express the fuel or energy value of food. Calorie values are determined by the content, in grams, of fat, carbohydrate, and protein. Technically the amount of heat energy needed to raise the temperature of 1000 grams of water (about 4 cups) by 1° C.

Carbohydrates.   Largely composed of sugars and starches, carbohydrates are one of the three basic food classifications, the other two being fats and proteins.

Cyclamates.   Artificial sweeteners that have now been banned. Saccharine may still be purchased and is listed on package and bottle labels when it is an ingredient.

Dehydration.   The removal of water, or the freeing of vegetables or fruits from moisture for purposes of preservation.

Dehydrofreeze.   To partially dehydrate food and quick freeze it for refrigerator storage.

Emulsification.   The process in manufacture of food products or in cooking that breaks down fat so that it remains suspended in liquid, as in the making of mayonnaise.

Enrichment. Foods that have been supplemented with minerals or vitamins according to federal laws. When processing depletes the nutrient values of a food, enrichments restore them.

Fats. Animal, vegetable, or synthetic fats come in solid or liquid form. They are one of the three basic food classifications and are essential to the utilization of some of the vitamins. Fat is a protector against changes in temperature and cold.

Fertilizers. Natural or chemically produced soil enrichers to promote growth. At present the nitrogen fertilizers (chemical) are largely taking the place of animal manures (natural).

Fortify. To add or strengthen the natural content of a food, as the addition of vitamin D to milk.

Fungicides. Chemical sprays used to prevent or destroy fungi.

Glazes. Substances used to coat food—to protect or enhance its appearance.

Grains. The edible seeds of the food plants—wheat, oats, rye, rice, corn, and buckwheat. They are called whole grains when they are unrefined. Grains are rich in carbohydrates and protein.

Granola. A homemade or commercially blended combination of oats, sesame seeds, honey, wheat, wheat germ, brewers' yeast, and optional nuts or other ingredients. Rich in proteins, it can be eaten dry or with milk as a cereal, or it can be used as a topping on other foods such as yogurt. A good basis for cookies.

Hydrogenation. A process that passes hydrogen through heated oils. It prevents rancidity, and fats treated in this way can tolerate high temperatures. It solidifies oils, while partial hydrogenation keeps oils liquid.

Insecticides.   Chemical substances usually sprayed on plants to destroy insects.

Minerals and trace minerals.   A group of inorganic sub-stances, including iron and calcium, that are essential to life. They are found in foods or can be supplemented.

Mold inhibitors.   Chemicals used to retard mold or spoilage of foods.

Nutrition.   The food or the process of feeding of humans, animals, and plants. The required nourishment to main-tain life, promote growth and energy, and replace loss.

Pesticides.   Chemical preparations for destroying insect pests. Used in spray, dust, and other forms.

Preservatives.   Chemical substances added to foods to pre-vent fermentation or spoilage, to prolong their life before and after purchase.

Processed foods.   Technologically treated foods as opposed to raw foods. The processing of foods moves them further toward what are now called the "convenience foods."

Processing.   The treatment and preparation of food—canning, freezing, drying, and pickling.

Protein.   One of the three basic food classifications, along with carbohydrates and fats. Protein forms body tissues and is the basis of all life. The complete proteins are the ones that can supply all the necessary protein in the diet. They are present in all foods that contain the 8 essential amino acids.

Starches.   The basis of most carbohydrates is starch and sugar. The starches in cookery are the pastas, potatoes, rice, and grains or cereals.

Supplements.   Additions supplied to fulfill a deficiency in foods. Supplementary proteins, vitamins, and other nutrients are available in various forms as tablets or powders, which should be taken only on medical advice.

Synthetics. Products resulting from technological develop-
ments in such foods as sugar, fruit juices, and several
protein foods. A laboratory product as opposed to a
naturally grown product.

Vitamins. Substances first isolated and designated in 1910
that are essential to life and growth. Vitamins A, D, E,
and K are grouped as fat soluble; vitamin C and the B-
complexes are water soluble. The vitamins are found in
natural foods or supplemented in the manufacture of
food products. They are also available in various forms
as a diet supplement.

Waxes. Wax or synthetic coatings used to enhance the appearance of certain foods. Also used to cover foods, e.g.,
on cheeses, or to coat food containers.

CHAPTER III
A Selective Guide to Health-Food-Store Shopping

Concern with well-being and proper eating is healthy and desirable unless it is exaggerated and becomes a fad. A fad can only be a temporary enthusiasm, and where health is concerned there is no room for passing fancies. If we want to achieve and maintain good health, we cannot concern ourselves with it one year and ignore it the next. Many people look upon their own well-being as though it were a life-long experiment, trying everything that comes along. Almost everyone wants to be something other than they are, either richer or healthier or thinner, and in the realm of being healthier and thinner they follow the latest "promise-full" book or the latest fad diet.

At the moment there is such a wave of awareness about health that it is rapidly becoming an industry. We have become concerned about the way in which our food is grown, preserved, and processed, and many of us have been alarmed by the facts—and the misinterpretations of them—to the point of losing a common-sense approach to our daily food needs. Some of us have become sufficiently apprehensive about the possible threats to health in the chemically grown and processed foods that we are marketing at the health-food stores that are springing up across the nation. This is remarkable because it usually entails some inconvenience and considerably more expense than regular supermarket buying.

There have always been health movements, herbalists, and health-food stores, and more recently there have been health publications. But they have never before existed on as large a scale, engaged as much interest, or been as financially successful. We do not know whether they are here to stay—but a publisher once said, include the word "health" in a title and the book will sell. The "health" industry is now worth nearly two billion dollars a year, and apparently it is going to become a real success.

As in many such cases, what the public complains about today is what they demanded a few years ago, and much of what they are now willing to pay for has been there all along. What health-food followers are now discovering has, indeed, always been at their disposal. It is a little dull to hear foods praised that many of us have always gone out of our way to buy, and foods condemned that many of us never ate to begin with.

The first thing to be said for the health-food movement is Bravo. It has made itself heard, and the American food industry has been quick to react—as it had to be. Within a very short time young homemakers no longer had to struggle over baking a healthy loaf of bread. The bread counter of the supermarket has a totally new look. There are whole-wheat loaves, imported whole-grain breads, and pumpernickels. Both Pepperidge Farm and Arnold have produced outstanding health breads. Pepperidge Farm's Sprouted Wheat Bread tastes as good toasted as it does plain. And the long, soft, porous, sliced white loaf is now no longer in first place on the market shelf.

We also have health-foods advocates to thank for the

granola products. Many adults who haven't touched a cereal for years have now discovered Crunchy Granola, Honey Almond, and High Protein Granola to eat and to crush and sprinkle over fruits and creams, as we once sprinkled crushed macaroons. We can also follow the recipe for granola cookies attached to the package.

Bread has always stood as a symbol of man's needs—and at times as a symbol of his prosperity. Most people have mistakenly demanded whiter and more refined breads, and those of us who didn't approve of them or didn't like them had to order stone-ground flours by mail or drive to one of the few old mills—like Sturbridge—that were still functioning. We also had to go to great trouble to buy rye and whole-wheat breads from small bakeries.

The new breads are only an example of what the "raised voices" have accomplished. Enriched white breads are at the moment in disrepute, but greater enrichment will soon place the white breads ahead of the whole-wheat breads. And so the public will benefit while the baking companies compete. Bread is only one example; progress is being made in many other fields.

The United States produces the best food in the world, but it is now under attack by a large and surprisingly young group of people. Young people usually take their health for granted—and disregard it accordingly—but now they have taken an interest, and that in itself is a healthy manifestation that is bringing about improvements.

There is no doubt that we are not eating as healthfully as we should, not because we cannot buy healthy foods, but because we have become shortcutters. We demand good looks in food and we follow the can-opener way without reading the labels. On top of all that, we eat too much.

We lean now toward the natural foods but there are some things that must be clearly understood before we can make a choice between marketing as we always have (but with more attention), marketing at the health-food stores, or combining the best of each.

Organically grown foods can only be produced in limited

quantities and are correspondingly more expensive. Ideally we should still have our farms and gardens and raise our own foods, but we have become an urban society and most of us can no longer grow our own food. If we want organic and natural food, we must either patronize the health-food stores or literally move to the remote country where water is unpolluted and where we can buy organically raised meat.

The health-food shop is the answer for the food purist. Well-stocked health-food stores have all the organic foods and natural foods along with cosmetics and pure beauty aids, goats' milk, natural cheeses, brewers' yeast, and organic cleaning materials. They carry the meat substitutes, salt-free products, herbal teas, and unpasteurized milk and butter. Their vitamins and honey, food supplements, and other nutriments are endless.

All health-food stores are rich in literature, with natural-food cookbooks, organic-gardening books, magazines and folders . . . but the most interesting thing at the health-food stores is the clientele. At one time the only patrons were faddists, but now there is an endless chain of young people. The owner of Panacea, a health-food store in New York City, says that 60 percent of his clients are under thirty years of age, and they are steady buyers of cheeses, health sandwiches, unpasteurized cream, goats' milk, raw sugar, dried fruits, nuts, and grains. Panacea's clientele does not consist entirely of housewives, as shown by their store hours—from 11:00 A.M. until 7:30 P.M. on weekdays and from 10:00 A.M. to 6:00 P.M. on Saturdays.

A well-supplied, clean, and reliable health-food store, or a health-food department in a supermarket or department store, carries products that should be used in every household. Many also carry appliances that are not available in all regular kitchen-ware departments, such as vegetable steamers, sprouters, and yogurt makers.

How to Select and Evaluate

It is hard to make a selection from the array of products offered by the health-food shops by relying on label information. The one thing that all the literature, folders, labels, and advocates have in common is enthusiasm. Many health foods, dairy products, eggs, and baked goods that should be dated are still sold undated. Catalogues are vague and the industry is so young that we are not yet familiar with all the manufacturers' names.

Owners of small health-food shops and their sales help can advise, but the best method of selection is to rely on appearance and common sense.

Do not buy products at the health-food shops or department stores that are available at the supermarkets. Prices should be lower at the supermarkets and turnover is probably faster.

Buy these *unsalted products* at health-food shops:

Butter
Vege-base soup base
Vegetable broth
Bouillon cubes (beef and chicken)
Peanut butter
Toasted peanuts
Shelled nuts, almonds, cashews, peanuts, and walnuts

Mayonnaise, only when homemade is not available
Cottage cheese .
Goats' milk cottage cheese
Breads
Cereals
Mustard
Pickles

Buy *oils, vinegar,* and *mayonnaise* at health-food shops only if they are not available at the market:

Sunflower-seed oil
Safflower-seed oil
Peanut oil
Coconut oil
Safflower-oil mayonnaise

Linseed oil
Soy oil
Sesame-seed oil
Cider vinegar

Buy the following *salts and seasonings* at a health-food store or specialty shop:

> Sea salt
> Vegetable-seasoning salt

Health-food shops or departments are a good source for some *breads,* although most markets now stock them, and for some of the *flours, grains,* and *yeast:*

100% gluten bread	Natural unbleached flour
Waerland bread	Whole-wheat flour
Soy and whole-wheat bread	Whole-wheat pastry flour
Thin or flat breads	Brown rice
Whole-wheat wafers	Wild rice
Whole-rye wafers	Raw or toasted wheat germ
Stone-ground flours without preservatives	Food yeast, nutritional yeast, brewers' yeast
Buckwheat flour	Cracked wheat
Rye flour	Bulgar wheat
Soy flour	

Buy *honey* only where it is stored at 50° F. or under.

The selection of *herbal teas* may be wider at a health-food store than at a regular market:

> Rose hip   Peppermint
> Wild rose hip   Hyssop
> Linden blossom   Alfalfa mint
> Camomile

The *vitamins, natural vitamins,* and *food supplements* available at health-food shops are so numerous and so confusing that it would be best to consult your physician about whether vitamins are necessary with your food regimen. Find out when and in what quantity to take them and do not be misled by promises. If your physician gives you a prescription, buy vitamins from your pharmacy.

This brings us to the *organic foods* and *natural foods*. The housewife should understand that no one can say whether every vegetable or meat labeled as organically grown is actually entirely so. The shopkeeper may offer the product in good faith, and his sources may be reliable and conscientious, but it would be impossible to institute a program of constant inspection. If the homemaker chooses to buy organic food, she must select an absolutely clean and apparently reliable dealer or shop. Needless to say big companies such as Sears, Alexander's, and many others have too much at stake to offer nonorganic foods under an organic label, however even there the housewife has to read and judge.

The American housewife who faces the question of health and the feeding of her family with common sense can do most of her marketing at any well-stocked market or supermarket or from reputable specialty stores. There is a wide choice of safe foods and the turnover is so rapid in most neighborhoods that she can be assured of buying fresh and properly stored foods.

Always remember that raised voices are healthy but fads can take on dangerous proportions. Two hundred million Americans cannot subsist as the early settlers did. The present upheaval is spurring on research and legislation and administration that will ultimately eliminate any possible perils. But American homemakers cannot stop the vast machinery of food production. What each one of us must do is study our own family's food habits and faults and remedy the errors we are making, rather than to go miles out of our way to buy a brown-sugar health candy.

CHAPTER IV
Menu and
Meal Planning

We should never abandon ourselves totally to the enjoyment of the good things in life, since it is only when we do not overdo them that we are capable of enjoying them. Remember that with every menu plan you make.

Menu-making at best is not easy. It has always presented problems to people who simply cannot *think* of food early in the day, or to others who try to plan meals for the week ahead on Monday morning. The old advice has always been: try to plan all meals when you are hungry and never go to market on a full stomach.

Adding to the difficulties of composing meals that will suit the preferences of the entire family, there is always the budget to keep in mind and the "specials" to watch out for at the market. An eye has to be kept on the kitchen appliances and equipment. It may be that two things cannot be roasted in the oven at the same time, or Tuesday may be washday. On top of all this we now must add two important considerations to all the menus we make, *health* and *weight* (really one and the same thing).

Every homemaker has kept health at the back of her mind in planning meals for her family, but only from the standpoint of getting the proper nourishment into her children—and possibly her husband—each day. She has never questioned the actual healthfulness of the food she bought. Now health has assumed a new meaning. The housewife is warned that she has to protect the health of her family from possible threats in the very foods that have seemed the most reliable. Her family still must be properly nourished, but now it has to be nourished with the foods that are unquestionably safe. It is not enough to think of bread pudding; now we have to think about the flour that went into the bread.

Just how grave the threats are we do not yet know, but the alarms have been sounded, and the warnings have brought about a change of attitude. As we have said, warnings are healthy. They show us that we are eating foods that may ultimately be detrimental to our well-being. Even more important, we have been eating those foods in combinations, in quantities, and in preparations that have been dangerously unhealthful.

Refined sugars may never have done us as much good as raw sugar or honey, but *too many sweets* have always been harmful. The menu-maker is being told to substitute brown sugars, raw sugar, or honey for refined sugars, but she is not being told that it would be much more beneficial to cut down on the amount of sugar in the daily menu. When weight is being watched, sugar must be cut down—not substituted. Do not use chemical sweeteners, unless they are prescribed by your physician, at a time when you are questioning the entire field of agricultural chemicals.

The moment that you become aware of the dangers of sugar, think of the *amount* you use. If you have been convinced that refined sugars may be harmful, then cut out at least half of them in your meal planning, and substitute the raw and brown sugars and honey for the other half. Your children will benefit much more from natural sugars in fruit and honey on their whole-grain breads than from another wedge of layer cake. Tea should never be sweetened at all. If unsweetened coffee tastes unpalatable, sweeten it very slightly or give it up entirely rather than using a chemical sweetener. We have mentioned earlier that it takes about a week to learn to prefer unsweetened tea and coffee. After that sweetened tea tastes like syrup and we wonder how we ever drank it. In the East, where tea drinking is a fine art, it is never sweetened (nor is it made bitterly strong).

Healthful menus are easy menus for the housewife—you need no longer break your head over who prefers chocolate cream pie or who wants lemon meringue, or whether there will be time to bake dessert or whether there will be something else in the oven. All these problems are washed away when you recognize that pie is a complete failure on the calorie count and contains both refined sugar and white flour. On top of that, eating a rich sweet with cooked fruit at the end of the meal is not nearly as beneficial as raw fruit at the beginning.

What we are trying to do in our menu-making is to sort out what may be harmful in the foods we purchase at the market and what foods may be harmful from a health standpoint, irrespective of their treatment or processing. We are also eliminating the less digestible forms of preparation— and that leaves the housewife with very simple menu-making and no problems at all. The resultant meals are more along the lines of what the intelligent epicure has been eating for generations—*fresh foods, simply prepared, from the best obtainable ingredients, eaten with enjoyment, at leisure, in moderation.*

Those perfectly simple rules cover the greatest cookery in the world and are based on the fundamental wisdom at the beginning of this chapter. The true epicure eats intelligently so that he can enjoy it more—and longer. The menu-maker today does not need imagination, she needs intelligence. She has to sort out all the values, but when she has worked out her daily repertoire, she will be better off in terms of health, finances, and time. The more time-consuming and complicated food preparations are, the less most of them contribute to our well-being.

The young menu-makers who want to go back to the foods of their great grandparents should remember that the standing rib-roast on Sunday tasted infinitely better at the end of a week of beefless meals than it tastes now after a week of alternating steaks, hamburgers, pot roast, and hash—and another steak on Saturday. I recently heard a woman described by a young guest in our home, who wanted to give me a clear picture in the language I would understand. He said she was the sort of woman who still served roast beef on Sunday. As far as he, who ate beef twice a day all week, was concerned, that was dull cookery. All of which was said just before we sat down to what I thought was a beautiful roast of beef . . . and it was a Sunday too!

A healthful menu is easier to make than an unhealthful one. The choice is smaller and we are not led down the by-ways of new prepared or canned products, since we aren't going to eat any more of them anyway. The following rules and suggestions should be remembered in making the menu and the marketing list.

How Much or How Little to Serve

Soups

1 scant cup per person. Always substitute the soup; do not supplement it to a full meal.

Vegetables and salads

Artichokes   1 serves 1 to 2
Asparagus   1 pound (16 to 20 stalks) serves 4

Avocado	1 serves 2
Beans, green	1 pound serves 5 at ½ cup each
Beans, lima	1 pound serves 2 at ⅓ cup each
Beets	1 pound serves 3 to 4
Broccoli	1 pound serves 3
Brussels sprouts	1 pound serves 4 to 5
Cabbage, white	1 pound (approximately ½ head) serves 4 to 6
Cabbage, red	1 pound (approximately ½ head) serves 4 to 6
Carrots	1 pound serves 5 at ½ cup each
Cauliflower	1 pound, about 3 to 3½ servings
Corn	1 to 2 ears per person, depending on size
Eggplant	1 pound serves 5 at ½ cup diced each
Frozen vegetables	(only if fresh are unobtainable) 10- to 12-ounce package serves 2 to 3
Lettuce	1 medium head serves 2 to 4
Mushrooms	1 pound serves 6
Onions	1 pound, 3 large onions, serves 3 to 4
Potatoes, white	1 pound, 3 medium potatoes, serves 2 or 3
Potatoes, sweet or yams	1 pound, 3 medium potatoes, serves 3
Spinach	1 pound serves 4 to 6
Tomatoes	1 pound, 4 small tomatoes, serves 4

Dried vegetables

1 pound dried vegetables, or 2½ cups, serves 8 at ¾ cup each

Meat

With bone	1 pound serves 2; large bone, 1 pound serves 1
Without bone, or ground	1 pound serves up to 4

Fish

Whole	1 pound serves 1
Drawn	1 pound serves 2
Steaks	1 pound serves 3
Clams and oysters	5 to 6 on the half shell serves 1
Lobster	1 pound serves 1
Lobster meat	1 pound serves 4 to 6
Shrimp	1 pound, about 16 to 20, serves 3 to 4

Poultry

Broiler	1 pound serves 2
Fryer	1 pound serves 2 to 4
Roasting chicken	1 pound serves 1 or more
Stewing hen	1 pound serves 1 to 3
Duck	1⅓ pound serves 1
Turkey	1 pound serves 1 to 2

Starches

Bread	1 pound, or 16 slices, serves 8 at 2 slices each per day
Rice	1 pound, or 2¼ cups, serves 12 to 14 at ½ cup each
Pasta	1 pound, or 4 to 5 cups, serves 7 at ½ cup each

Dairy products

Cottage cheese	1 pound, or 2 cups, serves 4 to 6
Milk	1 quart, or 4 cups, serves 6 to 8
Ice cream	1 quart, or 4 cups, serves 4 to 8

Children should eat between meals, but adults should not. Tea and other beverages should be drunk between meals but food should be confined to breakfast, lunch, and dinner or to breakfast, dinner, and supper. The traditional way to put on weight has been to eat between meals, to eat often, and to eat three meals a day besides. This is still a reliable way to put on weight. A coffee break or two, sweetened tea in the afternoon with cake, a glass of milk and a few cookies before going to bed is still the pleasantest way of getting fat. It may take time but results can be guaranteed.

Making the Menu

Feeding a family healthfully, sensibly, and economically depends on three interrelated steps: planning the meals, marketing for them, and preparing the food. The final meal is more easily prepared and less wasteful when each step is properly completed before the next one is taken. A meal cannot be planned as you wander down the market aisles. You cannot look for inspiration on the counters and shelves. It is possible to make a change when a "special" is well priced, but a basic plan has to be followed. The plan should be made for several days ahead so that leftovers can be considered. When menus are made to provide healthful nutrition it is best to make them weekly rather than daily, so that a rich sweet on Monday or a lean vegetable meal on Tuesday can be compensated for before the week is over. A weekly plan shows an overall picture and gives the menu-maker an opportunity to balance deficiencies or excesses.

It is certainly not necessary to count calories when meals are well balanced and properly organized. If you entertain guests on Saturday and then eat out several days in a row, it stands to reason that a few lean days must follow. The quickest way to eliminate overindulgences is to interrupt them and intersperse at least three lean days for every rich one.

The menu-maker is always told that her family needs a *balanced diet*. The easiest way for anyone who has not actually studied dietetics to accomplish a balanced diet is to introduce great variety, not only in foods served, but in their preparation. Broil, poach, braise, steam, roast, and bake the foods. Include raw and cooked vegetables and fruits. *And always remember that the protective foods are the whole-*

grain breads and cereals, milk, fish, meat, eggs, vegetables, and fruits.
Do not make rich or complicated concoctions. Increase portions if your family appears to need more, or decrease portions if anyone is putting on too much weight. Do not eliminate any of the foods and maintain variety in your menus at all times.

Breakfast

Breakfast is an important meal. Most nations that have given up many of their individualistic eating habits cling staunchly to their breakfast patterns. The English still have early—or bed—tea before breakfast, the Austrians have breakfast (coffee and a roll) and a fork breakfast later on. The Oslo breakfast includes cheese and in Denmark there is always Danish pastry. A very thin shaving of Gjetost cheese on dark bread with orange marmalade is a wonderful combination of English and Norwegian customs and a sustaining start for a cold and strenuous day.

Breaking our fast correctly is more important than we think. In the cool or cold countries and in winter, warm breakfasts are essential. It is no wonder that the Scots make such good porridges and the New Englanders started their day with hot griddle cakes. Weather no longer plays such an important part in our well-insulated homes, but it stands to reason that a bowl of cold, dry cereal will be more tempting in summer than on a cold winter morning.

Breakfasts, whether large or small, should always start with fruit—not a fruit juice, but fruit. There should also be a warm beverage; tea or herb tea are the most healthful breakfast beverages. For all active adults there should be eggs and/or bacon, and if possible breakfasts should be so satisfying that the morning coffee break will be eliminated. Breakfast should take care of about one fourth to one third of the essential daily proteins, vitamins, minerals—and calories.

Breakfast Menus

These are only suggestions of how much to serve and possible combinations. Any preferred foods may be eaten.

½ grapefruit
Toasted sprouted-wheat bread
Comb honey
Eggs, 1 or 2, and/or bacon
Plain tea

½ sliced orange
Whole-wheat bread
Apple butter
Crisp bacon
Plain peppermint tea

½ cantaloupe filled with berries and a few walnut halves
Poached egg or eggs
Toasted whole-grain bread
Plain camomile tea

Mixed berries with thick milk
Scrambled egg with chopped ham
Toasted whole-wheat muffin
Plain rose hip tea

Sliced peaches
Granola
Thin full-kernel bread
Crisp bacon or a leftover cold meat
Plain linden blossom or lemon tea

Raspberries with cream
Parched whole-wheat bread
Broiled liver
Tomato slices
Plain tea

In planning breakfast menus, remember that it is usually the first meal after about twelve hours' fasting, and it precedes another five hours of fasting before the next meal.

Breakfast tides the body over about seventeen hours of the day, while the gap between dinner and supper or luncheon and dinner is usually not more than six hours. The size of breakfast portions depends on the amount of activity. An active man needs two eggs and possibly a lamb chop, while an inactive man should not eat more than one egg.

Lunch

Breakfasts and dinners or suppers are usually normal meals, eaten at about the same time each day, but luncheon is irregular. Most men are at work or in the office, children are in school, and housewives use the midday meal either to diet or to fulfill social obligations. It is impossible to set down more than an outline for what luncheons should be.

Since meat is expensive and since we eat too much of it in any case, fruits, vegetables, and eggs should be eaten at lunch. If meals are reversed and dinner is eaten in the middle of the day, then supper should be the light meal.

The egg yolk contains B vitamins, is rich in vitamin A, and is a good source of vitamin D. High-quality protein is found in both the yolk and the white of an egg, and nutritionists rate eggs as one of our most important foods. They can be interchanged with poultry, meat, or fish when meals are being planned. Like other foods that are rich in protein, eggs can enhance the supplementary proteins in grains and vegetables when they are properly combined.

There are classic food combinations which do just that. They date back to a time when there was no knowledge of food values and were presumably eaten together because they tasted good. An example of this is hard-cooked egg on spinach. The egg increases the contribution of the vegetable protein, so menu-makers should plan to serve steamed spinach, spinach soup or salad with a general topping of riced or sliced hard-cooked eggs.

The egg is a versatile, healthy, and economical food that should not be limited to the breakfast menu. An egg sandwich is as valuable as meat on the luncheon menu, and an egg salad with fruit should satisfy the members of the family who are watching their weight. Unless your physician has put you on an eggless diet, eat at least one each day.

Luncheon or Supper Menus With Eggs

Grapefruit sections
Radishes and celery
Poached eggs on spinach
Lightly buttered oven-dried whole-wheat bread
Filberts and unsulphured dates and figs

Sliced peaches
Celery and carrot sticks
Zucchini and endive and hard-cooked egg salad
Buttered sprouted-wheat bread
Stilton cheese with apple slices

Sliced oranges with mint
Poached egg in bouillon
Parched whole-wheat bread chunks with parsley butter and
   homemade sour-milk cheese

Sliced tomato with chopped chives and watercress
Riced hard-cooked egg over cold cooked cauliflower with
   Lemon French Dressing
Seedless grapes with Brie cheese

Luncheon or Supper Menus Without Eggs

Syracusan Orange Salad
Squash with Toasted Almonds
Rye crisps
Green tea after luncheon

Iced Cherry Soup
Braised Endive
Whole-wheat melba toast
Plain tea with lemon after luncheon

Paradise Salad
Honey-glazed Carrots and Onions
Miniature whole-wheat muffins
Berries in season
Camomile tea after luncheon

Grapefruit sections with endive
Vegetables in Foil
Cheese and rye crisps

Cold Celery with Coulis
Applesauce
Granola cookies
Plain tea after luncheon

Melon wedge
Ratatouille
Warm whole-wheat bread
Honey butter

Tangerines
Eggplant Casserole I
Waerland bread or pumpernickel with lemon butter

Raw Spinach Salad
Toasted, buttered sprouted-wheat bread
Thick Milk
Eden Salad
Cheese rolls (whole-wheat bread rolled with chived cream
   cheese)

Strawberries
Flemish Salad
Pumpernickel with Camembert cheese
Plain tea after luncheon

Dinner

Although it is healthful to eat dinner or the main meal in the middle of the day, most of us are unable to do so. We eat our heaviest and most important meal in the evening and often retire shortly after eating it. The menu planner should try to relegate the heavier meats to Sunday dinner and serve light broiled meats and poultry on workday evenings. The following suggestions include fruits and vegetables to satisfy the appetite without relying on heavy stews, pot roasts, and expensive roasts. Whenever possible—for instance, during vacations—eat dinner in the middle of the day.

Dinner Menus

Grapefruit sections
Onion Soufflé
Whole-wheat melba toast
Broiled steak slices with watercress
Small new potatoes boiled in their jackets and shaken with
    dill butter
Bowl of unsulphured dried fruits and nuts

Chilled melon wedges with minced mint and lemon peel
Eggplant Casserole II
Broiled liver
Small baked potatoes with onion butter
Cheese and rye crackers

Green beans vinaigrette, with hard-cooked egg and minced
    onion
Lemon Chicken
Duchesse Potatoes
Mixed cold fruit
Granola cookies

Sliced oranges with minced green pepper and thinly sliced
    raw mushrooms
Cold Celery with Coulis

Skewered lamb
Stewed pears

Berries or fruit in season
Veal Chops in Packages
Steamed potatoes with parsley
Crème Brulée

Sutton Place Salad
Veal Chops on Applesauce
Parched whole-wheat bread
Biscuit Tortoni

Iced Apple Soup
Cold Chicken with Filberts
Whole-wheat popovers with cold honey butter
Red and green grapes with nuts and raisins

Cold fruit cups
Watercress Salad
Mushrooms with Brown Rice
Broiled steak

½ cantaloupe or melon in season
Leek and Potato Soup
Mixed green salad with Roquefort cheese

Orange and Endive Salad
French Dressing
Red Onion Soup
Toasted fresh rye bread
Applesauce

Brussels Sprouts with Seedless Grapes
Roast beef
Small baked potato
Hazelnut Pudding

½ grapefruit
Tomato and corn casserole
Cold chicken with aspic jelly
Apple Nut Pie

CHAPTER V

The Feeding of Infants and Children

The greatest progress in health has not been in prolonging the life expectancy of the adult, but in reducing the rate of infant and child illness. We have healthier babies and they grow into healthier young children for a combination of reasons: environmental, medical, generally improved health conditions, and better nourishment. Most infants are given a good start in life and show a surprising determination to thrive. They know exactly what they want and exactly when they want it, and all the parents have to do is fulfill their daily nutritional needs. There are excellent books on how to feed your infant or your growing children, but no books on how to implant a desire for healthful eating in your child. Their every natural instinct is to undo your good work from the moment they are old enough to get beyond your control and be on their own.

What every healthy adult needs is a well-nourished childhood, and while good foundations can tide the children over the years when they seem to subsist on snacks, pie, soda, potato chips, peanut butter, and hot dogs, the children cannot take the abuse forever. Parents have to teach their children respect for their health, but telling them that a nice green vegetable *is all for their own good* is not the way to do it. Feeding children properly for their better health while they are young and growing is only half the battle (and much the better half). Giving them a foundation of healthful eating habits that will last for the rest of their lives is the real objective.

Tastes and preferences are unexplained phenomena that crop up in the youngest children, long before they are old enough to reason why they love one flavor and hate another. Children show the first signs of rebellion while they are still in their high chairs (usually at the sight of a carrot or something that is equally good for them), and that is only the forerunner of all the future protests and tears with which they will resist the foods they do not like or the milk they do not want to drink. All of these struggles ultimately lead to the school-age splurges into unbelievable concoctions and combinations that were not allowed while they were under parental supervision.

When children dream of what they will do when they are grown up, it is almost always in terms of *forbidden foods,* usually sweet and indigestible, with which they want to express their freedom and independence. Every child envisions happiness as eating anything he wants, at any time (preferably in the middle of the night), anywhere, and in any quantity!

I remember that my own school life began with healthy milk and graham crackers, which changed to jelly sandwiches and cocoa as I grew older. After that came the first luncheon in the school cafeteria. I selected Lyonnaise potatoes and a four-inch-high white layer cake topped with two more inches of a white, marshmallowlike substance that was topped, in turn, by another inch of white shredded coconut. On the way home I spent the money that had been saved on meat and vegetables on a milk-chocolate almond bar. There was nothing very remarkable about that luncheon except that it was my first opportunity for making a free, unsupervised choice, and I ate that same luncheon every day, month in and month out, for the entire school year.

While the mother still has full control of feeding her child she should not look upon it as a daily routine that will be taken out of her hands in a few years. It should be a preparation for the child's entire adult life, not in terms of growing big and strong but in terms of having the right attitude toward food and health.

The Infant

The only news we want to hear about a newborn infant is that he is healthy. We know clearly at that moment (and forget it for the rest of our lives) that health is the only thing that really matters. From his first days the infant is fed the best, the most nourishing, and the purest foods that can be obtained. Everything is done to maintain and build the infant's health, and everything else takes second place to the importance of keeping the baby strong and well. Then, within a relatively short time the child takes over and makes his tastes felt. He doesn't want variety, he doesn't want cereal, and in no time at all he has developed a strong set of likes and dislikes. The parents gradually give in (because it is easier) and eating habits are formed around *taste*, which is probably the least valid means of selecting a healthy diet. The fact that the child's health was once a cause for jubilation is forgotten . . . what we lose is not the energy and perseverance to maintain good health in our children as they grow older, but the memory of its importance.

A newborn infant requires more than twice as many calories per day, per pound of body weight, as an adult. The scale decreases through childhood and maturity, depending on activity and bodily conformation, but the infant who has only resting needs requires as many as 24 to 50 calories per pound. A 10-pound baby will need 500 calories per day while its 120-pound mother will need only about three times as many.

Your infant's nutritional needs should be guided by your doctor and pediatrician. Climate (summer heat and winter cold) is a factor, for instance, that cannot be taken into account in a book. The generally recommended dietary needs of an infant are:

Water. Two and one-half ounces per pound per day is a general rule. A water deficiency can be harmful, so the proper amount of water has to be adjusted to climate and other needs.

Calories. During the first months of life the infant needs more than 50 calories per pound per day. Toward the end of the first year, when growth begins to slow down, the daily calorie need decreases gradually.

Protein. Two grams per pound per day are recommended for the artificially fed infant. Breast milk contains sufficient protein.

Fat. Infants do not tolerate high-fat diets, but low-fat milk may cause a deficiency in vitamin A. As in all matters of infant feeding, check with your pediatrician.

Carbohydrates. All milks contain carbohydrates, and there is no necessity for supplementation in the average infant's formula.

Calcium. Thirty mg. per pound per day is desirable. The artifically fed infant gets its daily requirement in its milk. Breast-fed infants get less calcium without apparent harm.

Phosphorus. Like calcium, this mineral is sufficiently present in all milk.

Iron. Six mg. daily are recommended after the first few months. It is present in the cereals and meats that should be started at this time.

Vitamin A. Milk usually contains enough vitamin A to

satisfy the daily recommendation, but your pediatrician may advise additional amounts, which can be given with vitamin D.

Vitamin D. This must be added to the infant's diet.

Vitamin C, ascorbic acid. Thirty mg. daily are recommended and should be added to the milk diet.

Riboflavin and niacin. Milk contains sufficient riboflavin, and niacin deficiency does not occur in normal infants.

The Daily Formula

Depending on where you live and your pediatrician's advice, the daily formula may be purchased or constructed. The infant's needs must be determined, and changes and additions have to be made from time to time.

The infant's daily needs are: 50 calories per pound of body weight

2 grams protein per pound of body weight

2½ ounces water per pound of body weight

Milk contains: 20 calories per ounce

1 gram protein per ounce.

Therefore 2 ounces of milk will contain 40 calories and 2 grams of protein. In practice this means that the formula should consist of approximately 2 ounces of milk per pound of body weight per day with an addition of ½ ounce water per pound each day and approximately 2 tablespoons sugar or syrup for each quart of the milk-and-water mixture. Milk satisfies most of an infant's nutritional needs for the first six months, with vitamins D and C and iron added. The formula must be given in small amounts to begin with and gradually increased to larger amounts as toleration is established.

Solid Foods

These can be started when the infant is about three months old, or when he is consuming about one quart of milk per day. Cereals, cooked egg yolk, and sieved meat provide iron in sufficient quantity. Cereal is usually the best starter and can be fed from a very small spoon before the morning bottle. If the infant rejects it, try again next day, and continue to try until he accepts it. In time a second solid food can be added to the diet before the supper bottle, but only in very small amounts. When the infant has become accustomed to solid foods, a greater variety should be given until he eats small quantities of solid foods before each bottle. When the baby is about six months old, chopped foods can be substituted for the sieved and pureed foods.

Feeding Errors

Feeding problems usually arise out of feeding errors. The most common ones are: the mother's misestimation of how much food her baby should eat, her belief that her baby should eat the same amount at the same meal every day, and her idea that meals must remain on a rigid time schedule. What every mother should understand is that feeding the growing baby is not force-feeding the growing baby. The baby's growth and appetite will slow down, and he will eat as much as he needs. As he grows older he will develop new diversions and interests, and his sole aim in life will no longer be his bottle. He will require relatively less and less—not more and more—food as the months go by.

Another grave danger is that mothers unconsciously impose their own food tastes on their babies. Any show of dislike on the parents' part is felt by a clever baby, and while he doesn't reason, he acts. If mother makes a face over his infant food he will reject it. Trained infant nurses used to call all baby's food lovely; they raved about it while they fed him, and baby grew in the happy illusion that his porridge was divine. *No food should ever be forced on an infant or baby,*

*and as he grows he should only be given as much as he will
eat.* If there is a real eating problem that does not arise out of
mother's wrong ideas, see the pediatrician at once.

The Growing Child

Each day's food for the growing child should include 3 to
5 cups fluids and 2 to 3 cups milk (counted in the fluids) or
other milk products such as cottage cheese or ice cream. There
should be 1 to 2 servings of meat, chicken, fish, or eggs and
1 to 2 servings of green and yellow vegetables. Add 1 serving of citrus fruit or tomatoes and 1 serving of potatoes. There
should be 1 to 2 servings of cereal, 1 to 2 of bread, and at
least 2 tablespoons of butter. The child's diet must supply
him with protein, calcium, iron, and vitamins A, C, B_1, B_2,
and B_3. In terms of calories, children need the following:

Children (boys and girls)

Age	Approximate Weight	Approximate No. of Calories
1	20	1050
3	30	1250
5	40	1600
7–8	50	1800
8–9	60	2000
9–10	70	2200

There isn't a mother who has not told her child that he
must drink his milk to *grow big and strong,* and there isn't a
child who listens or cares. Parents feed their children for the
future, not only for their future health but for their future
attitude toward their health. Children have to be taught an
awareness and respect for keeping well by eating well without making them overaware. The child does not exist who
will ask for two vegetables and a glass of milk when mother
isn't around, but the good eating habits that began in the

high chair and the growing years are the ones that he will swing back to as an adult, hopefully before serious damage is done. All bad eating habits should be broken before they settle in. Children lean toward oversweetening and over-seasoning and overdousing their food with hot, spiced sauces. They copy the adult who sprinkles salt over his food before he tastes it and then washes it down with an icy beverage. They rarely copy good eating habits and they have to be steered away from the bad ones before a pattern is established.

Some parents fail at the difficult task of teaching their children to eat properly, through their own fault. Small children and animals eat instinctively when they are hungry and stop eating as soon as their appetite has been appeased. They feel no obligation whatever to finish what is on their plates. They can still hear that built-in signal that tells them when they have eaten enough . . . which adults unfortunately grow deaf to. Mothers often force their children to eat beyond the point of satiation because there is food left in the bowl or on the plate, but the amount that was put there to begin with (by the mother) was arbitrarily arrived at without actual consideration for the child's capacity. In the matter of quantity, children often know better than their mothers.

When a child does not finish the food on his plate, try giving him less until eating the entire meal has become an established habit. Then increase the amounts gradually to conform to the *proper* daily requirements. If the child rejects the added food, put in a pleasant food-break between meals. When children can be made to *enjoy* the foods that are good for them, they won't abandon them the moment they are away from home. Unless the habit of sensible eating is deeply rooted, the high-school and college years usually superimpose a poor pattern of food preferences that is more apt to last through the adult years than the earlier, more healthful regimen. Parents should never let children associate their meals with haste, scoldings, unpleasantness, or forced feeding. One of the rules of healthful eating for adults is to chew well, eat slowly, and not to eat under tension or stress. The same rule holds good for the children. Eating will become an adult pleasure, so it might just as well start as one for the children while they are young. They should always look forward to their meals, and parents should make them something to look forward to.

From Twelve to Eighteen

Teenagers	Age	Approximate Weight	Approximate No. of Calories
Girls	12–14	90	2400
	14–16	100	2500
	16–18	110	2600
Boys	12–14	80–90	2500
	14–16	100–110	3000
	16–18	120+	3000

The need for protein, calcium, iron, and vitamins A, C, B_1, B_2, and B_3 increases with the greater demands of growth and physical exercise. The same foods should be maintained through the "teen" years. There should be 3 to 5 cups milk or milk products, such as cheese or ice cream, daily and 3 to 4 servings of meat, poultry, fish, or eggs. Add 2 servings of green and yellow vegetables, 2 servings of citrus fruits and tomatoes, and 1 serving of potatoes. There should also be 4 to 6 servings of cereals and bread and at least 3 to 4 table-spoons butter.

As with adults, teenagers' daily requirements depend on size of frame, amount of activity, participation in strenuous sports, and climate. During these years when parental super-vision is low and fad-eating is high, healthful eating is more essential than ever. Nagging is no help, however, and par-ents have to sit by while their active, growing children dip indigestible fried foods into hot sauces and wash them down with ice-cold soda. If they have a "barge" or a "float" or any of their favorite things, they get their calories—probably too many—without getting the required nutrients, but if parents try to lecture on malnutrition among the young (where there is both education and enough income) they won't listen.

There is only one answer. Make home meals so good, so pleasant, and so appealing that they will stay home, bring their friends, and establish good habits. When refrigerator raiding becomes the style and your children toy with their food at the table and then eat you out of house and home at night, fill the refrigerator with good, healthful food that will also be a temptation. For every pint of ice cream, put in a loaf of sprouted-wheat bread. Nuts and dried fruits can take the place of salty snacks, and cold milk can look very good when there is a jar of brown sugar cookies at hand. Some of the new cereals—Granola, for example—taste as good as candy, and the recipe in the folder which accompanies the bag of cereal makes wonderful cookies.

Breakfast

Breakfasts for children should include fruit, milk, a whole-grain cereal, toast, jam, possibly a strip of bacon or an egg, and anything else they have a reasonable craving for. In Oslo children are given fruit, thinly sliced cheese, a piece of flaky pastry, milk, and dark bread with a spread containing disguised cod-liver oil. If the pink-cheeked Norwegian children are any indication, this is the perfect breakfast. It has become so popular throughout Scandinavia that it is known as the Oslo breakfast, just as we recognize griddle cakes and maple syrup as the New England breakfast.

For children breakfast should be the most important meal of the day. This is particularly true after they have reached school age and expend an enormous amount of energy before noon—when they rush through part or none of their lunch box instead of buying and eating the lunch provided at school. The child's minimum food requirements per day are almost as large as an adult's and should be spread across *three* meals. They cannot be crowded into the remaining two. The child will not watch out for nutritional values at lunch, and dinner—at the end of a strenuous day and shortly before going to bed—is not the time for a large meal. Breakfast should be the time for milk products, cereal, fruit, butter, an egg or bacon or both—but instead most children hastily swallow a little dry cereal (and leave most of it behind) before they tear off for school.

Children see their fathers depart for work on a swallow of coffee. A large majority of the sedentary office workers stop at a counter on their way to work, where they have a cup of coffee and some pastry. A depressing number of adults do not even stop to sit down; they go to the take-out counter and arrive at the office with a brown paper bag in which there is a paper container of sweetened coffee and a doughnut or something equally indigestible.

The office, plant, or shop may be miles from home—but the younger generation always manage to pick up their parents' bad eating habits. I was appalled to hear of—and see— a comparable breakfast activity going on in a junior way at the corner newspaper store in a suburban town. The children, who had left their breakfasts uneaten at home, were getting their preschool ice-cold soda, candy, and packaged snacks before going on to class. Bad eating habits seem to have something for every generation.

Here, as in most cases having to do with the eating habits of the young, the parents are largely to blame. Most of us know how hard it is to get children out of bed. Cooking a large, tempting, well-balanced breakfast and then getting them to eat it is almost more than some parents can cope with —especially in competition with the charms of a cold coke and a chocolate bar at the corner store.

The answer is always the same . . . make breakfast at home so good and so pleasant that the children establish the habit of eating it there. If a boy between nine and ten needs at least 2200 calories a day, his breakfast should contain *milk* or a *milk product*, a *high-protein food* such as egg or bacon, a *citrus fruit*, a *cereal* or *bread* (preferably both), and *butter* or *margarine*. The sugar in the fruit, the possible jam or honey on the bread, and the possible sugar in or on the cereal is enough; there is no need for that candy bar or any other sweet at the corner store.

Variety in breakfasts is always essential. The milk product can change from the usual glass of milk to yogurt. Cottage cheese can alternate with Strawberries and Devonshire Cream, page 224. The Oslo breakfast cheese can be wonderful on a slice of black bread with orange marmalade. The citrus fruit can be orange sections one day, one-half grapefruit the next, and homemade tomato juice on another day.

The high protein food can be an egg or eggs in any form, bacon, peanut butter, or one of the cheeses (when cheese does not represent the milk product on that particular day).

The breads and cereals present countless variations and possibilities. There can be corn bread, whole-grain breads, a whole-wheat muffin, waffles and buckwheat pancakes, dry or cooked cereals. Granola cannot fail to tempt.

Butter or margarine is usually a spread for the bread at breakfast, and honey, jams, and marmalades come in such a wide choice that there can be variations for every day of the week.

Breakfast Menus

Orange sections
Granola with cream
2 slices toasted sprouted-wheat bread
Butter and natural comb honey
Egg nog

½ grapefruit
Shredded wheat with brown sugar and cream
Scrambled eggs with crumbled bacon
Slice of tomato
Toasted whole-wheat muffin with orange butter
Milk

Homemade tomato juice
Cornmeal pancakes with maple syrup
2 slices crisp bacon
Yogurt

Make a chart of what each child should eat each day and juggle the essentials to give them variety and interest. Feeding a child properly is the first consideration in bringing him up properly, and making the food attractive and tempting is the easiest way of getting it eaten.

Lunch

If a good proportion of the daily nutritional requirements have been eaten at breakfast, then luncheon should supply poultry, meat, or fish, cooked and raw vegetables, and more of the essentials that were eaten with breakfast. School-lunch programs are composed by dieticians and should give all the necessary foods, but children are apt to eat only part of them, and if they do not fall within the narrow limits of the children's preferences, they will not succeed. Many children prefer a school-box lunch, which their mothers should make tempting and appetizing. Fortunately there are endless possibilities for the ever-popular sandwich. It can contain the important meats, poultry, fish, eggs, or cheese. The bread supplies essential nourishment, but it should not dominate the filling. Fruit, cookies, surprises, and goodies are more apt to be eaten, because parents are more aware of taste preferences than the dietician.

Mothers can count on their children "snacking," and they can prevent the useless snacks by supplying the useful ones. A few can be put into the lunch box, others can be strategically disposed around the house when the children come home from school. Among all the other advantages of doing this, money can be saved.

The container industry has made it possible to wrap, bag, contain, and present any form of food without a lot of spilling and spoiling.

Sandwich Luncheons

Turkey and tomato sandwich on whole-grain bread
Sliced apple salad with granola in a small container
Peanuts and raisins in a small bag
Milk (in a thermos or bought at school)

Sliced cheese on sprouted-wheat bread
Coleslaw with raisins in a small container
A banana and whole-wheat cookies
Milk

Egg-salad sandwich on pumpernickel bread
Celery and carrot sticks
Orange sections in a small container
Granola almond cookies
Milk

Peanut butter on rye bread
Crisp bacon strips
Strawberries with cream and chopped walnuts in a small
   container
Cold vegetable juice

Norwegian Gjetost cheese on whole-wheat bread with
   orange marmalade
Granola cookies
Apple
Milk

Hamburger on whole-wheat bun
Sliced tomatoes and homemade relish in a small container
Oatmeal cookies
Milk

The above suggestions may be extreme in the eyes of a
child who wants to conform with all the other children. It is
up to the mother to make slight changes and additions to the
lunch box until a healthful, varied luncheon is established.

A mother should not let the child's wish to eat exactly like
all his classmates lead her into putting a salty slice of lunch-

eon meat between two slices of white bread and adding a piece of bought cake.

Supper

If the child's luncheon was a sandwich then supper should not be another. Supper menus depend largely on family arrangements. If parents and children can eat together then the children should eat their parents' varied diet as soon as possible including, of course, fruit, vegetables, proteins, and milk.

If it is impossible for children to eat with their parents during the school year, then supper should be a warm meal containing the meats and vegetables that were not eaten in sufficient quantity at lunchtime. If the children eat a warm lunch, supper can be the sandwich meal. If it is possible to arrange, the larger meal at noon and the lighter meal in the evening is to be preferred.

Snacks

The average adult does not need food between meals but the average child does. Snacks do not have to be eaten at a set time, but they should be there to satisfy the sudden appetite or thirst. Nuts, raisins, unsulphured dried fruits, whole-grain cookies, fruit, brown-sugar confections (not too many), and honey all make good snacks. So do wonderfully crisp homemade parched nuts and similar temptations. Avoid the highly salted or spiced or deep-fat-fried commercial products, iced soda, candy bars, and all the novelties that find their way into small cellophane bags or boxes, for which millions of dollars are spent each year.

Children should not eat or drink when they come hot and breathless from playing. They should not be scolded or lectured while they eat. They should eat slowly (not too slowly) and chew well, and all meals at home should be as nicely presented as possible. Getting them to eat a more varied diet may take time, but don't give up—their health and their attitude toward food are still in your hands.

CHAPTER VI

Food Preparation, Useful Hints, and Recipes

Most of us have been eating the results of our cooking for years, and we are accustomed to the general pattern of preferences we have established, which, taken en masse, constitute the "Consumer Tastes" of the nation. We have used ingredients, day in and day out, that we now consider detrimental to health. We have also become accustomed to staples such as bleached flour, refined sugar, and polished rice that may not be actively detrimental but do not serve a constructive purpose in building up resistance and good health. Now we are understandably eager to know what to substitute for them.

Since we are likely to eat such staples in restaurants or at the homes of our friends, it is wise to be doubly vigilant at home. The following recipes are for household use—for healthful eating and for dieting when it is necessary. Positively desirable ingredients have been substituted for the

74

negative ones, which—since they are not actively beneficial—were merely fillers.

All these recipes stand up to the test of delicacy . . . there is no purpose served in recommending dishes that taste less well than the ones to which we are accustomed, since we are bound to return, in the end, to the things that taste better.

This is not a group of fad recipes. No carrot cake or soybean loaf will be forced on a temporary dieter. It is a collection of recipes for the epicure who eats well, wisely, and healthfully, with no white sauces or flour thickeners, no deep-fat-fried food, and no artificial sweeteners. Study these recipes and live by them for a time until they become a habit. When you cook out of your own recipe file or out of any cookbook, select only those recipes which follow this general pattern.

The resultant regimen is actually no different from the repertoire of the sophisticated food lover who has learned to prefer his meat with its natural juices instead of with a floured gravy, who prefers a strong consommé or a pureed vegetable soup to a heavy cream soup thickened with flour. The sensible gastronome—even in Paris—will always gravitate to the lighter desserts, fruits, and cheeses.

A healthful eating regimen asks no sacrifices, nor will it make you young, rich, and beautiful overnight, but in the long run it will make your weight adjust to normal (by loss or gain) and give you a lovely sense of well-being and freedom.

Cooking Rules

Certain general rules in cooking and eating healthfully apply to all recipes. We list them here for you to remember from now on. They can be applied to your present menus, to your existing recipes, and to your possible dieting:

1. Never peel potatoes. Scrub them and bake, steam, or boil them in their skins. If a recipe calls for a peeled potato, as in potato salad or potato soup, draw off the thin

skin *after* the potato has been boiled and while it is still warm.

2. Steam homegrown, organically grown, or sun-ripened, market-fresh vegetables in a little water; do not boil unless vegetables are old and hard. See vegetable steaming chart on page 141.

3. For all weight-loss dieters and sufferers from arthritis and many other maladies, it is necessary to reduce or omit salt from the diet. The following recipes are prepared without salt, but can be salted to taste in the usual way. If the recipes are prepared with salt or if you add salt after cooking, *use less* than you have used in the past. Omit it wherever possible. Unsalted food tastes bland at first, but after a few weeks the natural flavors of the foods emerge and become stronger. *Never salt food before tasting it,* and then only use salt if it is absolutely necessary. Use sea or Maldon table sea salt or one of the natural salts.

4. Broil, roast, steam, boil, poach, grill, or pan-fry meats, poultry, and fish. Do not fry them in deep fat or bread them before frying. Do not dredge with flour.

5. Drink little or no liquids with meals; drink them between meals instead. Adults should always think of milk as a food and not as a beverage. Substitute it for another food—have a glass of milk *instead* of soup. Do not drink milk *besides* the regular full menu. Children do require milk besides their regular foods.

6. Use natural full-kernel grains. No white flours are used in the following recipes, which does not mean that a slice of white bread would hurt you. It just wouldn't help you as much as a slice of whole-wheat or full-kernel bread.

7. Sweeten with honey, for health, digestibility, and flavor. Cut down on sugar and use brown sugars, raw sugar, Barbados sugar, or maple sugar. Do not make honey syrups for stewing fruit because boiling honey destroys most of its benefits.

8. Use butter, clarified butter, bacon fat, or natural fats. Margarine is not recommended for cooking. Use olive, corn, sunflower, or safflower oils.

Menu Rules

1. Always eat fruit, salad, or vegetables at the beginning of a meal. Do not serve fruit or vegetable juices.

2. If soups are eaten, substitute them for another course. Do not add them to a full meal.

3. Serve butter or egg sauces, mayonnaise, or Hollandaise, but do not serve gravies or sauces thickened with flour.

4. At least half the food at main meals should consist of raw fruit and vegetables, and only *half* of the vegetables should be cooked. Salads, celery, carrot sticks, and radishes should be included at all main meals.

Eating Rules

1. Never eat unless you are hungry and stop eating when your appetite is appeased.

2. Never eat when tired, emotionally upset, tense, or depressed.

3. Eat slowly and chew well.

4. Do not wash down solids with liquids.

The foods and beverages that are conspicuously absent from these recipes are, we regret to say, not healthful for average household menus. They are not necessarily harmful, and in some climates or for very active persons they are desirable, but those are the exceptions. The man in Spitzbergen knows that he needs oils and foods that the man on the equator doesn't, and the active country sportsman needs more food than the sedentary city dweller, but most of us require a less rich, less fattening diet.

More vegetable and salad recipes are included than ways to cook meat, since most Americans are natural meat eaters but have, until recently, neglected the vegetables—raw and cooked.

What Your Pantry and Refrigerator Should Include

Breads	Crisp Finn, Kauli, and other Norwegian crisp or flat breads, Scotch oatcakes, unsalted French rusks (biscotte), wheat thins, sprouted-wheat or whole-wheat bread
Cereals and grains	Crunchy granola, wheat germ, familia (Swiss bircher muesli), honey almond crunch, and Scotch oatmeal
Fats	Butter, lard, natural fats, e.g., bacon or chicken fat
Flours	Whole-wheat, natural unbleached, rye, stone-ground and corn meal
Honey	Comb, granulated, or strained
Milk	Fresh, dried, skimmed, buttermilk, or cream
Oil	Olive oil, corn oil, sunflower oil, or safflower oil
Rice	Natural brown
Salt	Sea salt, Ischl, Maldon, or imported Sel de Mer
Sugar	Raw, brown, Barbados, Demerara, or maple
Teas	Black or green, camomile, linden blossom, rose hip, mint, and other herb teas
Vinegar	Apple cider or fruit vinegars only

SALADS AND RAW FOODS

The recipes in this book are arranged in order of their most helpful menu rotation. Salads should be eaten before the main course, as is the custom in the western United States. Many nutritionists and physicians now recommend that the meal start with fruit or a vegetable or fruit salad. The salad appeases the appetite, and especially when weight is being watched, it is a very easy way of controlling overeating. Many restaurants throughout the United States place the salad on the table first of all, and many diners are satisfied before they reach the dessert.

Salads

As *raw vegetables* are an essential part of at least one meal a day, the salad course should include them, or they should be served separately *at the beginning of the meal*. Celery and carrot sticks, radishes, cucumber and zucchini strips, fennel, and raw cauliflower can be served at all meals without dressing. Salads can also include all the varieties of lettuces, watercress, avocado, cabbages, young peas, spring onions, peppers, tomatoes, kohlrabi, fresh herbs, and spinach as well as cold cooked vegetables.

Cooked salad vegetables include potatoes, beets, cauliflower, celery root, peas, beans of all kinds, artichokes, asparagus, leeks, and eggplant.

A healthy salad should contain variety: a root vegetable, a leaf vegetable, and a fruit vegetable (one that grows over the ground)—or, as an old theory puts it, a good salad has to have three colors.

Root Vegetables	Fruit Vegetables	Leaf Vegetables
Beets	Peas	All lettuces
Carrots	Beans	Endive
Kohlrabi	Tomatoes	Spinach
Celery	Cauliflower	Watercress
Radishes	Cucumbers	Red cabbage
All onions	Zucchini	White cabbage

Salad Dressings and Mayonnaises

FRENCH DRESSING

½ teaspoon sea salt
⅛ teaspoon freshly
    ground black pepper

¼ cup tarragon vinegar
¼ cup olive oil
½ cup peanut oil

Stir the salt and pepper with the vinegar until the salt is dissolved. Add the oils and shake or beat well before serving.

ROQUEFORT DRESSING

Add 3 tablespoons crumbled Roquefort or Blue Cheese to 1 recipe French Dressing and shake well before serving.

LEMON FRENCH DRESSING

4 tablespoons lemon juice
¾ teaspoon sea salt ·
¼ teaspoon paprika
¼ teaspoon freshly
   ground black pepper

¾ cup peanut oil
2 teaspoons chopped mint
2 teaspoons chopped parsley
1 clove garlic

Stir the salt, paprika, and pepper with the lemon juice until the salt is dissolved. Add oil, herbs, and garlic and shake well. Remove the garlic before using.

BACON DRESSING

4 strips chilled bacon,
   cut into dice with
   kitchen scissors

1 tablespoon butter
⅛ teaspoon freshly ground
   pepper

¼ cup tarragon vinegar

Fry the bacon in the butter until just golden. Take from heat, add pepper and vinegar, and stir well. Pour the warm dressing over the prepared salad greens and serve at once.

FRUIT SALAD DRESSING

½ teaspoon sea salt
⅛ teaspoon white pepper
2 tablespoons fresh lime
   juice

2 tablespoons fresh lemon
   juice
¾ cup safflower
   oil

1 tablespoon chopped mint or parsley

Stir salt and pepper into fruit juices until salt is dissolved. Add oil and mint. Add an ice cube, shake or beat well until thick and smooth. Remove the ice cube.

BLENDER DRESSING FOR WEIGHT-LOSS DIET

3 tomatoes, peeled, sliced, and seeded
1 small onion, sliced
½ cup cider vinegar
1 teaspoon dried herbs: oregano, chervil, basil, or dill
4 black peppercorns
½ teaspoon sea salt, optional
¼ teaspoon dry mustard, or to taste
6 sprigs parsley, stems removed

Place all ingredients in blender container and blend until smooth. Chill. Serve over lettuce greens, tomatoes, zucchini, cauliflower, or mushrooms. Sprinkle with additional chopped parsley.

CREAM DRESSING

½ teaspoon sea salt
⅛ teaspoon freshly ground black pepper
¼ cup cider vinegar or lemon juice
¾ cup heavy cream

Stir dry ingredients into the vinegar or juice until the salt is dissolved. Add the cream and shake or beat well before serving.

GARLIC DRESSING

1 garlic clove, stuck with a wooden toothpick
⅔ cup cider vinegar
1 teaspoon sea salt, or to taste
¼ teaspoon white pepper
1½ cups peanut oil

Put garlic clove into a jar with vinegar and dry ingredients and set it aside for 1 week. Add the oil and shake well. Take out the garlic and refrigerate the dressing until needed.

CELERY SEED DRESSING

½ teaspoon sea salt
1 pinch black pepper
½ teaspoon mild brown
   mustard
1 tablespoon minced
   onion

1 ice cube fresh from the ice
   tray
¾ cup oil
¼ cup tarragon vinegar
1 teaspoon celery seed

In beater mix salt and pepper with mustard, add onion and ice cube and beat in the oil, drop by drop, as for mayonnaise. When the sauce thickens, beat in the rest of the oil in a thin stream, add the vinegar and celery seed and serve at once.

ITALIAN DRESSING

½ teaspoon sea salt
¼ teaspoon freshly
   ground black pepper
⅓ cup tarragon vinegar
⅔ cup olive oil

1 tablespoon minced onion
1 tablespoon minced herbs:
   Italian parsley, oregano,
   and basil
2 teaspoons minced pimento

1 small garlic clove, minced

Stir salt and pepper into the vinegar until the salt is dissolved. Beat in the oil and remaining ingredients and let the dressing "draw" in the refrigerator overnight. Shake well before serving.

RUSSIAN DRESSING

1 cup mayonnaise
1 tablespoon parsley,
   minced
2 tablespoons Tomato
   Sauce

1 tablespoon green pepper,
   finely chopped
1 tablespoon pimento finely
   cut
½ tablespoon chives,
   finely chopped

Fold all together and serve.

HONEY DRESSING
FOR FRUIT SALADS

2 tablespoons honey
1 teaspoon mild brown
  mustard
¼ teaspoon sea salt
1 pinch pepper
¼ cup cider vinegar

1 tablespoon minced
  shallots
1 ice cube
¾ cup safflower, soy, or
  peanut oil
1 tablespoon minced parsley

Stir honey with mustard, add salt and pepper, and stir until smooth. Add vinegar and shallots and shake well. Add the ice cube, oil, and parsley and shake well before serving.

ELECTRIC BEATER MAYONNAISE

Bring oil and other ingredients to at least 70° to 75° F. before making mayonnaise.

½ teaspoon dry mustard   2 teaspoons cider vinegar
½ teaspoon sea salt   2 egg yolks
            1 cup peanut oil

Set beater at low and beat dry ingredients with vinegar and egg yolks until smooth. Add the oil, drop by drop, from the tip of a tablespoon until the sauce starts to thicken, then add about ¼ tablespoon at a time, and when the sauce is very thick, add the rest of the oil in a thin stream. Chill the mayonnaise before using it. The most economical quantity to make is based on 2 egg yolks and 2 cups oil. It can be stored in a closed container in the refrigerator.

MUSTARD MAYONNAISE

To 1 recipe Electric Beater Mayonnaise, add ½ tablespoon prepared brown mustard after the oil has been incorporated. Beat only long enough to mix well.

BLENDER MAYONNAISE

1 whole egg	½ teaspoon sea salt
1 tablespoon tarragon	½ teaspoon dry mustard
vinegar	1 cup peanut oil

Put egg, vinegar, salt, and mustard in blender container, cover and blend for 10 seconds. Take off top and add oil in a thin stream, continuing to blend. When all the oil has been added, turn off motor and stir mayonnaise with a rubber scraper. Blend for 5 seconds longer and chill before serving.

BLENDER LEMON MAYONNAISE

1 whole egg	Grated rind of the whole
1 tablespoon fresh lemon	lemon
juice	1 cup peanut oil

Put egg, lemon juice, and rind into blender container, cover, and blend for 10 seconds. Take off top and add oil in a thin stream. When all the oil has been added, turn off the motor and stir mayonnaise with rubber scraper. Blend for 5 seconds longer and chill before serving.

MAYONNAISE VARIATIONS

Add the following ingredients to 1 cup mayonnaise:

Astoria Mayonnaise. Beat ½ cup French dressing into the mayonnaise, add 2 tablespoons strained chili sauce, 1 tablespoon minced onion, and ½ tablespoon minced green pepper.

Chantilly Mayonnaise. Fold ¼ cup heavy cream, stiffly whipped, into the mayonnaise just before serving.

Cream Mayonnaise. Stir ¼ cup heavy cream, half whipped, into the mayonnaise.

Green Mayonnaise. Mince 4 fresh spinach leaves with 2 parsley sprigs, all stems removed, and 1 tablespoon each cut chives and chopped pistachio nuts. When the mixture is reduced to a paste, stir it into the mayonnaise.

Honey Mayonnaise. Beat 1 tablespoon honey into the mayonnaise for fruit salads.

Lime Mayonnaise. Beat 1 tablespoon lime juice into the mayonnaise for fruit salads.

Norwegian Mayonnaise. Stir 2 tablespoons finely snipped fresh dill into the mayonnaise for fish, cucumber, cauliflower, or tomato salads.

Onion Mayonnaise. Fold 1 tablespoon minced spring onions and 2 tablespoons finely cut chives into the mayonnaise.

Roquefort Mayonnaise. Beat 3 tablespoons creamed Roquefort cheese into the mayonnaise, or blend in 3 tablespoons crumbled Roquefort cheese while making the mayonnaise.

Sour Cream Mayonnaise. Beat ½ cup homemade sour cream until light and smooth. Fold into the mayonnaise and add ¼ cup chopped pistachio nuts or walnuts.

Vincent Mayonnaise. When fresh herbs are available, fold ½ tablespoons each minced tarragon leaves, chives, chervil, parsley, and borage into the mayonnaise. Add ¼ cup chopped watercress leaves and 2 hard-cooked egg yolks, riced.

THOUSAND ISLAND DRESSING

1 tablespoon cider
  vinegar
⅓ cup homemade sour
  cream, whipped
1 hard-cooked egg, yolk
  and white riced
  separately

1 tablespoon minced green
  pepper
1 tablespoon minced onion
1 tablespoon minced parsley
1 tablespoon minced chives
2 tablespoons chili sauce
1 recipe mayonnaise

Combine all ingredients and fold them into the mayonnaise. Chill before serving.

CAMBRIDGE SAUCE

2 hard-cooked egg yolks,
    riced
1 teaspoon mild brown
    mustard
½ teaspoon sea salt
1 pinch pepper

1 cup peanut oil
¼ cup cider vinegar
2 tablespoons minced herbs:
    parsley, chervil, dill,
    tarragon, chives, or any
    combination

1 teaspoon minced capers

Crush the yolks with mustard and stir until smooth, add salt and pepper, and beat in the oil, drop by drop, as for mayonnaise. Stir in the vinegar, herbs, and capers, and chill the sauce until it is served.

Salad Recipes

In the following salad recipes the treatment of some of the ingredients is left to the housewife's discretion—namely the peeling of apples, tomatoes, and mushrooms. Much of the nutritional value of certain fruits and vegetables lies just under the skin; on the other hand, however, some peels are tough and not everyone can digest them. Mushrooms should not be peeled if they are clean or can be cleaned with a soft, damp cloth. If they are very scarred and brown they should be peeled and the ends should be trimmed from the stems.

PARADISE SALAD

3 large eating apples,
    peeled, cored, and cut
    into thin wedges
4 tomatoes, peeled and cut
    into wedges

Lettuce leaves
2 tablespoons brown sugar
French Dressing

Arrange alternating wedges of apples and tomatoes in a spiral on lettuce leaves on a salad platter. Sprinkle brown sugar over them and pour French Dressing carefully over the sugar just before serving.

STAR EGG SALAD

1 Boston lettuce, cleaned   18 cooked asparagus spears
  and trimmed   8 raw spinach leaves,
6 hard-cooked eggs, sliced   cleaned and shredded
            ½ cup Onion Mayonnaise

Cut head of lettuce into sixths and flatten out in a salad
bowl to form a star. Cut out the heart. Arrange overlapping
egg slices on the six lettuce points and put asparagus spears
between them. Center the salad with shredded spinach and
put the lettuce heart on it. Pass Onion Mayonnaise separately.

GERMAN SALAD

6 large potatoes, boiled,   2 hard-cooked eggs, yolks
  skinned, cooled, and   and whites riced
  cubed   separately
2 tart apples, cored and   1 recipe Cambridge Sauce
  diced   Boston lettuce leaves
1 dill pickle, diced   2 tablespoons chopped
½ medium onion, finely   parsley
  diced

Prepare and combine potatoes, apples, pickle, and onion in
a large bowl. Stir the riced yolks into the Cambridge Sauce.
Mix the salad with the sauce and place in a lettuce-lined
bowl. Sprinkle the salad with riced egg whites and parsley.

FRUIT SALAD ALICE

4 spears endive, trimmed   ½ pound sour cherries, pitted
  and sliced across   1 recipe Fruit Salad Dressing
1 grapefruit, sectioned with   or Honey Dressing
  membranes removed   Boston lettuce leaves for
2 oranges, sectioned with   bowl
  membranes removed   ½ green pepper, seeded and
1 sour apple, cored and cut   finely diced
  into very thin wedges

Combine the endive and fruit in a salad bowl. Surround with lettuce leaves, pour dressing over salad. Sprinkle with green pepper and serve with a platter of cheeses.

SYRACUSAN ORANGE SALAD

6 oranges, peeled and
  sliced across
2 onions, cut across into
  very thin slices
⅓ cup chopped walnuts
½ cup olive oil

1 pimento, finely diced
3 tablespoons minced parsley
3 black olives, diced (optional)

Slice the oranges over the salad bowl to catch all the juices. Arrange the orange slices alternating with the onion slices on a salad platter and chill. Fry the walnuts slowly in the oil until they are golden. Pour the warm oil and nuts over the cold salad, sprinkle with pimento and parsley, and serve at once. Diced black olives may be added to the pimento.

FLEMISH SALAD

6 medium potatoes,
  boiled, skinned,
  cooled, and sliced
3 heads Belgian endive,
  trimmed and sliced
  across
½ cup French Dressing,
  or to taste

2 onions, steamed, cooled,
  and sliced
6 parsley sprigs, stems removed
½ cup mayonnaise
Boston lettuce leaves

Combine potatoes and endive in a bowl, turn carefully with dressing, and chill. Put onion slices and parsley in a bowl and chop them together until fine. Before serving turn the salad once more with the mayonnaise and transfer it to a lettuce-lined salad bowl. Cover it with the mixture of onions and parsley.

LOUISIANA SALAD

Rub salad bowl with garlic. Line it with lettuce leaves and place 1 pound of freshly cooked and chilled shrimp in the center. Around them arrange small alternating mounds of raw and cooked vegetables: 1 cup cooked baby lima beans, 2 thinly sliced raw baby zucchini, and cooked cauliflower roses. Add 2 sliced tomatoes and 4 or 5 freshly sliced raw mushrooms. Pour Lemon French Dressing over the salad and serve Lemon Mayonnaise sprinkled with cut chives in a separate bowl. Cold cooked salmon may be substituted for the shrimp.

BABY LIMA BEAN SALAD

6 cups freshly cooked
baby lima beans,
drained and cold
½ onion, minced
½ cup diced bacon, fried
until crisp and drained

1 tablespoon chopped fresh
basil
½ cup Cream Dressing, or
to taste
3 tablespoons chopped parsley

Combine beans, onion, bacon dice, and basil. Add dressing and turn the salad gently. Sprinkle with parsley and serve.

WATERCRESS SALAD

½ Spanish onion, thinly
sliced
1 cucumber, scored and
sliced paper thin
3 tomatoes, thinly sliced

1 bunch watercress,
washed and all coarse
stems removed
⅔ cup French Dressing
¾ cup whole-wheat bread-
crumbs
2 tablespoons butter

Arrange alternating slices of onion, cucumber, and tomatoes in salad bowl. Surround them with watercress and add the dressing. Fry the breadcrumbs in butter until golden and spread them over the vegetable slices.

SUTTON PLACE SALAD

1 head Boston lettuce, cleaned and separated into leaves
3 stalks Belgian endive, trimmed and sliced
6 large mushrooms, trimmed and thinly sliced
2 zucchini, thinly sliced
3 small tomatoes, sliced across
Italian Dressing
2 hard-cooked eggs, sliced

Combine lettuce, endive, mushrooms, zucchini, and tomatoes in a large salad bowl. Add dressing and mix gently. Cover top with egg slices.

DIJON SALAD

4 large potatoes, cooked, skinned, cooled, and cubed
3 large cucumbers, peeled, seeded, and diced
1 recipe Mustard Mayonnaise
Lettuce leaves
1 bunch celery, trimmed, scraped, and sliced
½ cup French Dressing
¼ cup chives, chopped

Prepare potatoes and cucumber dice and bind them with Mustard Mayonnaise. Transfer the salad to a lettuce-leaf-lined salad bowl. Marinate celery slices in dressing, arrange them around the potatoes and cucumbers, and sprinkle the top heavily with chives.

ASPARAGUS SALAD

2 pounds asparagus, trimmed, steamed, and chilled
Boston lettuce leaves
3 hard-cooked eggs, sliced
1 onion, finely chopped
6 sprigs parsley, finely chopped
1 pimento, finely chopped
French Dressing

Arrange asparagus on lettuce leaves, lay an overlapping row of egg slices across the stalks and arrange a line each of chopped onion, parsley, and pimento on each side of the eggs. Serve with French Dressing in a sauceboat.

RAW SPINACH SALAD

1 pound fresh spinach, washed

2 sweet apples, peeled, cored, and sliced across paper thin

12 slices cold bacon, cut into dice with kitchen scissors

4 tablespoons tarragon vinegar

Remove coarse stems from cleaned spinach. Put spinach in a salad bowl with the sliced apples and chill. Fry bacon until golden, take it out with a slotted spoon, and drain well. Add to the salad. Sprinkle vinegar over salad and just before serving pour over the warm bacon fat.

UNDERGROUND SALAD

3 beets, steamed, scraped, and sliced

2 carrots, scraped, sliced, and boiled

2 potatoes boiled, skinned, and sliced

4 radishes, sliced

1 onion, sliced

½ head iceberg lettuce, shredded

Celery Seed Dressing

Carefully combine the sliced vegetables in a salad bowl. Surround with a border of shredded lettuce and pour Celery Seed Dressing over the salad.

EDEN SALAD

2 sour or green apples, peeled, cored, and diced

1 ripe pineapple, cut into chunks

2 potatoes, boiled, peeled, and diced

1 bunch celery, trimmed, scraped, and cut across into thin slices

½ bunch watercress, washed, with coarse stems removed

1 recipe Fruit Salad Dressing

½ cup chopped walnuts or hazelnuts

Combine the fruits with the potato and celery. Arrange the salad in a bowl, surround it with watercress, and add the minted dressing. Sprinkle salad with nuts and serve very cold.

Raw Foods

For many of us the foods we eat have become just as unnatural as the way we live. We lead sedentary, indoor lives, and we live almost entirely on cooked and processed foods. Health depends first of all on nature, so the more natural foods we eat the better. One of the first steps toward a healthier life is to introduce more *raw foods* into our diets. Vitamins are present in fruits and vegetables that are not in other foods, and many of them are more easily absorbed from these natural sources than in the form of pills. Although the fat-soluble vitamins are not lost in boiling or steaming, the water-soluble vitamins, the B-complex and C, may be partly lost when food is cooked in water. Because raw food is always crisp and dry, thorough chewing is part of its beneficial effect.

One of the rules for healthier eating is that half our daily food must consist of fruits and vegetables. Furthermore, half of those fruits and vegetables that we eat each day must be eaten raw. By raw we mean just that—*the natural must always be left just as natural as possible.* The raw foods most of us eat at present are limited to fruit juice (usually processed) or a little fresh fruit, an occasional celery stalk or radish, or a salad.

Salads are absolutely essential to healthful eating, but many salad ingredients are cooked. Other beneficial effects are partly offset by highly seasoned dressings or by long immersion in water. If greens are cut before they are washed, the water will absorb the minerals and part of the vitamins we need. When we do eat raw vegetables we often salt them or actually dip them in salt. The amount of salt that clings to one moist celery stalk is about as much as we should consume in a whole day—about ¾ teaspoon. Because vegetables contain natural mineral salts, they are among the few foods for which salt can be reduced or omitted without pain.

Both raw, uncooked foods *and* salads should be included each day in all healthful menu planning. All fruits, vegetables, and nuts can, theoretically, be eaten raw but some adapt themselves better than others. The best are:

Carrots	Mushrooms
Cauliflower	Parsley
Celery	Radishes
Cucumbers	Scallions and spring onions
Fennel	Tomatoes
Green peppers	Zucchini

If you have a vegetable garden this list can be increased to include very young peas, baby lima beans, and kohlrabi. The most healthful fruits and vegetables are freshly picked, so if possible grow your own or buy from a farm that sells home-grown products.

We should remember that our grandparents' dinners invariably began with celery, carrot sticks, and radishes. Furthermore, they had almonds or nuts at each place at the table. In time this was abandoned because it was too much trouble, and few housewives today make the effort to clean celery, curl carrots, or cut radishes into roses.

We do not know whether our grandparents started their meals with raw food and nuts as a conscious health measure, but we do know that the custom should not have been dropped. A few restaurants still serve these raw foods, but for the most part they are considered rather old-fashioned—some people even call them rabbit food. We now know that they are essential in a healthy diet and that *the proper place for them is on an empty stomach at the beginning of a meal.* We know that breakfast should begin with raw fruit; the other meals should start the same way or with the other raw foods.

How to Prepare Raw Foods

We need not shape or carve vegetables. All that is necessary is that they be washed—or scrubbed—and cut into suitable-sized pieces. Ideally, they should be prepared as soon before eating as possible, but since few of us have that much time, they can be prepared and stored in the refrigerator. There, they play an important part in all healthful eating because raw fruits and vegetables are the only perfect fillers for the *weak moments* that come each day. They are a boon when weight loss is important and a healthy way to tide over children and adults to the next meal.

Rinse or wash all fruits and vegetables *before* cutting them. Do not salt them or store them in salted or sugared water. Serve them cold and crisp. If raw foods such as sliced mushrooms, zucchini, or cucumbers do not seem palatable without salt, substitute a natural sea salt for table salt. Gradually reduce the quantity of salt used until the foods' natural flavors become recognizable and salt can be dispensed with.

For a change, raw foods can be used in various combinations and mixed with other ingredients. In these combinations they can become an entire meal, and for inactive dieters they can be the full menu on one raw-food day a week. Other recipes using uncooked fruits and vegetables with dressing or mayonnaise can be found under Salads.

Raw-Food Combinations

1. Thinly slice 1 bunch radishes and combine with 2 diced apples, the juice and grated rind of ½ lemon, and 1 cup grapefruit sections.

2. Finely chop 1 bunch radishes with ½ bunch watercress and sprinkle the mixture over sliced oranges.

3. Combine grapefruit sections with finely chopped green peppers and thinly sliced mushrooms.

4. Mix various fruits with raisins and toasted nuts or toasted oatmeal or granola.

5. Pour the juice of 2 oranges over 1½ pounds hulled strawberries, add grated orange rind and 2 tablespoons chopped walnuts.

6. Pour the juice of 1 lemon over 6 sliced peaches and add ¼ cup finely chopped almonds or hazelnuts.

7. Sprinkle orange and grapefruit sections with chopped cauliflower, cut chives, and slivered orange rind.

8. Combine 2 cups sweet apples with ¼ cup finely chopped onion, the juice of 1 lemon, and a topping of ½ diced red pepper mixed with ½ cup chopped walnuts.

9. A bowl of raw foods on shaved ice can contain:
    Carrots, scraped and cut into sticks
    Cauliflower, divided into small roses
    Celery and fennel, scraped and quartered
    Cucumber and zucchini, sliced lengthwise
    Green peppers, seeded and sliced paper thin
    Mushrooms, stems trimmed and caps thinly sliced
        down through the stems
    Parsley and watercress, rough stems removed
    Radishes, scallions, and spring onions, trimmed
    Tomatoes or cherry tomatoes, whole or sliced

10. All raw foods can be combined with cream, sour cream, yogurt, or whipped cream.

By eating these raw foods at the beginning of a meal, their benefits are quickly and totally absorbed. They satisfy the worst pangs of hunger, so less is eaten during the rest of the meal. If they are eaten late in the meal or at its end, the body no longer has the strength to absorb all the important elements they contain, and valuable nutrients are lost.

RAW CAULIFLOWER SALAD

1 medium cauliflower	1 tablespoon grated horse-
Juice of 1 lemon	radish, optional
½ pint yogurt	1 tablespoon minced parsley
2 tablespoons oil	or cut chives
¼ cup chopped toasted almonds	

Submerge the trimmed cauliflower in water, head down, for 1 hour. Separate into very small roses and arrange in a salad bowl. Sprinkle at once with half the lemon juice. Whip the yogurt with oil, horseradish, and parsley and pour mixture over the cauliflower. Sprinkle with almonds and serve.

RAW CABBAGE SALAD

1 small white cabbage
3 tablespoons lemon juice
2 apples, peeled, cored,
   and cut into match-
   sticks

¼ cup toasted whole-wheat
   breadcrumbs
¼ cup finely chopped pea-
   nuts
½ cup heavy cream

3 tablespoons oil

Shred trimmed cabbage *very fine*. Put shreds in a salad bowl and work with the back of a wooden spoon until soft. Add lemon juice and apples. Whip breadcrumbs and peanuts into the cream and gradually add the oil. Pour the sauce over the cabbage shreds and marinate for about 1 hour before serving.

EGGS AND CHEESE

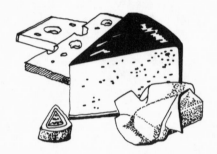

At the end of a small, serious, authoritative book on weight reduction in which all foods appeared to be either uninteresting or forbidden, I found the information that all other foods not mentioned could be eaten. A careful rereading revealed that the only *other* foods were eggs and cheese. They are good separately or together, in cold or hot dishes, and can be made into main luncheon dishes. The only time when cheese should not be eaten is *after* the dessert, but it is the perfect substitute to eat *in place* of the dessert.

SCRAMBLED EGGS WITH SOUR CREAM AND CHEESE

6 eggs   3 tablespoons grated cheese
½ cup sour cream   2 tablespoons butter

Beat eggs, sour cream, and cheese well. Melt butter in a wide pan, pour in the eggs, and cook them over medium heat until they begin to set. Gather them slowly toward the center of the pan until all are scrambled. Serve at once with hot, buttered whole-wheat toast.

SCRAMBLED EGGS WITH SHRIMP

8 fresh eggs	24 small shrimp, peeled, de-
A little pepper to taste	veined, and simmered for
3 tablespoons butter	4 minutes

3 tablespoons finely cut chives

Beat the eggs with a rotary beater just before scrambling them. Melt 2 tablespoons butter in a wide pan over medium heat and tilt the pan to cover the whole surface and edges with butter. Beat eggs for an instant and pour them over the butter before it sizzles. Let them "set" for a moment, then start gathering them toward one side of the pan as they thicken. Add the shrimp and 2 tablespoons chives and continue to draw egg mixture to one side of the pan until cooked and creamy. Stir in remaining butter and serve eggs with the remaining chives sprinkled over the top. Serve with tomatoes or a green salad.

SCRAMBLED EGGS WITH MUSHROOMS

8 fresh eggs	3 tablespoons butter
A little white pepper	1 cup fresh mushrooms,
3 tablespoons chopped	thinly sliced
parsley	

Beat the eggs with the pepper and parsley with a rotary beater. Melt half the butter in a wide pan, add the mushrooms, and fry them for a few minutes until they are just wilted. Pour off the mushroom liquid, add the remaining butter, and as soon as it is melted, beat the eggs once more and pour them over the mushrooms. Gather the egg mixture to one side of the pan as it cooks, continuing until cooked and creamy. Serve with a green bean salad. Use sea salt to taste if the flavor is too bland.

SCRAMBLED EGG VARIATIONS

Additional ingredients are either added to the eggs as they are scrambling, as in Scrambled Eggs with Shrimp, or they are fried in the pan just before the beaten eggs are added, as in Scrambled Eggs with Mushrooms. The following additions are for 8 eggs; reduce the quantity for fewer eggs.

With Onion. Fry ¼ cup chopped onion in butter until it is puffed and transparent, add the eggs, and scramble as above.

With Herbs. Add 2 tablespoons minced herbs, parsley, dill, chervil, and/or tarragon to the beaten eggs before scrambling.

With Chives. Add 2 tablespoons finely cut chives to the beaten eggs before scrambling and sprinkle 1 tablespoon finely cut chives over the finished eggs.

With Ham. Add ⅔ cup finely diced ham to the beaten eggs before they are scrambled.

With Croutons. Toast 1½ cups small cubes of stale whole-wheat bread in the oven with 2 tablespoons butter. Stir half the croutons into the eggs while they are scrambling and sprinkle the other half over the top of the finished eggs along with 2 tablespoons chopped parsley.

With Pimento and Green Pepper. Stir 1 chopped pimento and ½ green pepper, seeded and diced, into the beaten eggs before they are scrambled.

With Asparagus Spears Jeanette. Beat ¼ cup heavy cream with the eggs and mound the finished scrambled eggs across freshly cooked, hot asparagus spears.

HARD-COOKED EGGS I

Slide room-temperature eggs into boiling water with a slotted spoon. When water returns to a boil, cook for 12 minutes. Take pot from heat and hold under cold running water for a minute, then leave eggs in cold water until they are cold. Shell them carefully and return them to cold water until needed.

HARD-COOKED EGGS II

Put room-temperature eggs into ½ inch cold water in a saucepan. Cover the saucepan well and bring the water to a fast boil. Reduce heat and simmer eggs for 20 minutes. Take from heat, crack eggs and place them in a bowl of cold water.

POACHED EGGS

6 fresh eggs   1 tablespoon vinegar

Bring water to a boil in a shallow pan. Add vinegar and reduce heat so that the water bubbles but does not roll. Break one egg at a time into a saucer and "slip" into the water. Let eggs poach until the whites are firm and the yolks have disappeared, about three minutes. Remove with a slotted spoon. Drain eggs well, trim edges, and serve at once. If they have to be "held" for a few minutes, put them into warm water until needed. For cold poached eggs let them cool in cold water.

SIX-MINUTE EGGS

Six-minute eggs, or Eggs Mollet, are cooked in their shells in water until the white is just set but the yolk is still soft. Put room-temperature eggs into boiling water and boil for exactly 6 minutes. If they are to be eaten warm, peel them at once, carefully, and serve immediately. If they are to be served cold, they should be plunged into cold water the moment they are taken from the heat and held in cold water until ready to serve. As six-minute eggs can be used interchangeably with poached eggs in the following recipes, they are listed here and not with boiled eggs.

ANDALUSIAN POACHED EGGS

6 cold poached eggs
6 tomatoes, each large
  enough to hold an egg
1 cup mayonnaise
Boston lettuce leaves

Chopped parsley
1 onion, sliced paper thin
1 envelope gelatin
1¼ cups clear beef stock

Cut off top third of tomato to create a case for the eggs and a shallow shell for the mayonnaise. Scoop out meat and seeds and drain well. Put the poached eggs into the 6 deeper sections and divide mayonnaise over the 6 shallow sections. Sprinkle the mayonnaise with chopped parsley. Refrigerate the 12 filled tomato sections. Stir gelatin into ¼ cup stock. Bring the rest of the stock to a boil and take from the heat. Stir in the gelatin mixture until it is dissolved and pour into a wide pan to cool. It should be about ¼ inch deep. As soon as it is cool, let it set in the refrigerator, then cut into dice with a sharp knife. Serve the filled tomatoes on lettuce leaves garnished with onion rings and surround them with the diced aspic.

POACHED EGGS OR SIX-MINUTE EGGS
IN BAKED POTATOES

6 large baking potatoes
1½ onions thinly sliced, or
  8 shallots chopped

5 tablespoons butter
6 freshly poached or boiled
  eggs

Bake scrubbed potatoes in a 450° F. oven for 40 minutes or until soft and done. Sauté onion slices in butter until wilted and separated into rings. Cut lid from hot potatoes. Scoop out enough pulp to make a cavity. Partly fill with the wilted onions or shallots and the butter in which they were cooked. Cover onions with the poached eggs and serve at once with a crisp green salad.

Poached or six-minute eggs can also be served in any of the following ways for healthy meals:

Eggs Florentine: Lay eggs on a bed of fresh spinach cooked with a little heavy cream. Pour more cream over the eggs and sprinkle generously with grated Parmesan cheese. Put under a hot broiler for a few minutes to brown the cheese.

Eggs Argenteuil: Serve hot eggs on freshly cooked asparagus spears and cover with Mousseline Sauce (Hollandaise into which a little whipped cream has been folded, page 176).

Eggs Bearnaise: Place freshly cooked eggs on hot artichoke bottoms and cover with Bearnaise Sauce, page 175.

Norwegian Eggs: Serve hot eggs on well-drained pieces of boiled cod and pass browned butter mixed with chopped parsley.

Eggs Chantilly: Put freshly cooked eggs on a puree of fresh green peas and pass Mousseline Sauce. Serve triangles of toasted whole-wheat bread.

Eggs Zingara: Put freshly cooked eggs on slices of buttered toast, surround with lightly sautéed sliced mushrooms, and serve with a freshly made tomato sauce sprinkled with chopped parsley.

Cold Poached Egg with Watercress: Arrange cold eggs on thick slices of cold chicken, with sauce made of mayonnaise mixed with finely chopped watercress and thinned with heavy cream.

Cold Poached Eggs with Broccoli: Arrange cold eggs on cooked broccoli spears, cover with Lemon Mayonnaise, page 85, and sprinkle with chopped raw cauliflower.

CHEESE AND APPLES

1 Camembert cheese at   2 large tart apples, peeled
    room temperature   and chopped
          ½ cup chopped fresh watercress

Mash cheese and rind until smooth. Mix with chopped apples and watercress and serve with lightly buttered pumpernickel bread. Substitute for a sweet dessert.

CAMEMBERT CHEESE WITH PEARS

1 Camembert cheese, at   ¼ cup toasted wheat germ
    room temperature   6 tablespoons butter,
10 slices whole-wheat   creamed
    melba toast   6 ripe pears
            ¼ bunch watercress

Crush the whole-wheat toast and mix it with the wheat germ. Scrape the rind from the cheese, spread the top and sides with soft butter, and press the crumbs into it. The cheese should be completely covered with crumbs. Serve with pears and garnish with watercress.

HOMEMADE COTTAGE CHEESE

Make this when there is soured or clabbered milk available.

1 quart sour milk
          ¼ cup heavy cream, or to taste

Optional additional ingredients:

1 teaspoon grated onion   ½ teaspoon chopped caraway
1 teaspoon finely cut chives   seeds
            2 tablespoons mayonnaise

OR

2 tablespoons mayonnaise   2 tablespoons finely chopped
1 tablespoon minced onion   stuffed olives
1 tablespoon minced capers   1 tablespoon minced parsley

Heat sour milk in the top of a double boiler over simmering water until it is lukewarm, or 95° F. The milk will look as though it is about to curdle. Take from heat and let stand in a heating oven or a warm place for 10 minutes. Turn it into a cheesecloth laid across a strainer and let drain. Pour a pitcher of cold water through it and let drain completely again. Tie the ends of the cheesecloth firmly and hang over a bowl. Let the whey drain off until the curd is dry. Stir cream into the dry curd to taste and chill. Add any optional ingredients and serve.

SOUPS

Soups are healthful eating if they are not too salty, and if they are not an *addition* to the meal. To build a meal around a soup, eat a salad first, then a good soup, and then fruit or cheese. Or start with the fruit and end with salad and cheese. As soon as the soup becomes the major course of the meal, it gains in importance and usually gains in delicacy and ingredients—no one would want to create a meal around a watery broth! Since soups thickened with flour are not on the health regime, we substitute pureed vegetable soups (with the aid of a blender) and soups thickened with gelatin, cream, or egg yolks. Also included are cold fruit soups, dried vegetable soups, and healthful, strong vegetable or meat stocks for dieters.

Soup Stock

Homemade soup stock should be the basis for all soups. The canned soups are strong and the bouillon and consommé are clear, but they are all highly salted and are on many forbidden lists, especially where high blood pressure is being controlled. Bouillon cubes are also highly salted, but they are preferable to canned bouillons in an emergency. Homemade soup stocks can be as strong and as clear as you want to make them and they have the advantage that you know exactly what went into them.

Buying and preparing the ingredients for a strong, healthy soup stock takes a little time, and you have to stay home for four to six hours while it simmers. But beyond that it requires no special talent.

Stocks—chicken, beef, fish, or vegetable—are the unclarified liquids obtained by boiling the ingredients in water.

Bouillon is the French term for stock or broth and describes the liquid in the stockpot or kettle.

Consommé is the enriched and reduced stock that has been clarified.

ABOUT CHICKEN STOCK

Chicken stock is usually made by simmering a fowl and vegetables in water. The meat of the fowl can then be ground or minced to use in some recipes, but the flavor and strength have been boiled out of it. If you plan to use the chicken for a fricassee or similar dish, it should be put into already boiling water, which seals in the juices of the chicken.

When a whole chicken is being broiled or roasted, a small quantity of good chicken stock should be made out of the neck, wing tips, and giblets. Put them up in 3 cups cold water with a carrot, a slice of onion, and a sprig of parsley and bring them to a boil. Skim off the scum, reduce heat, and simmer covered until the water is reduced to half. Strain and use for sauce, or add it to your stock of chicken stock.

CHICKEN STOCK

1 5- to 5½-pound fowl, disjointed	3 carrots, scrubbed and quartered
1 pound veal knuckle bones or soup bones, cracked	2 onions, stuck with 2 cloves 4 stalks celery, with leaves ½ bay leaf
3 quarts fresh cold water	6 to 8 sprigs parsley

1 sprig thyme

Optional ingredients:

2 leeks, trimmed to white part only	2 sprigs chervil Sea salt to taste
1 turnip, peeled	3 to 4 peppercorns

Place well-cleaned fowl and soup bones into a large soup kettle, add water, cover, and bring to a boil. The slower it comes to the boiling point the better. At intervals lift off the scum that rises to the surface with a slotted spoon. When the water reaches the boiling point, add the well-cleaned vegetables and herbs. Cover the kettle, reduce heat, and simmer slowly for 3½ to 4 hours. Some cooks start with 1½ quarts water and add ½ cup cold water every hour. After 3½ to 4 hours the stock will have reduced considerably, so add water only if necessary. The more reduced the stock, the more nourishing and tasteful it will be. Use the chicken meat for a chicken mousse or sandwiches.

If preferred, all ingredients may be put into the kettle from the beginning. Add cold water and bring slowly to a boil. Lift the scum, cover the kettle, and reduce heat to simmer.

The stock can be made into consommé or bouillon by clarifying and reducing it for additional strength. The strong clarified consommé or bouillon is suitable for all jellied soups and the more delicate purees.

TO CLARIFY THE STOCK I

1 recipe chicken stock
2 egg whites, lightly
  beaten

2 eggshells, broken or
  crushed

Chill stock and lift off the fat. Stir stock and the clarifying agents—egg whites and shells—together in a clean kettle. Set over heat and bring slowly to the boiling point, stirring constantly and slowly. As soon as the boiling point is reached, reduce heat and simmer uncovered and undisturbed for 30 minutes. Lift the gathered sediment from the soup with a slotted spoon and strain the soup through a triple cheesecloth wrung out in cold water and laid across a strainer. Repeat straining 2 or 3 times if necessary.

TO CLARIFY THE STOCK II

Lift fat from 1 recipe cold chicken stock. Boil uncovered until it is reduced to half. Chill the reduced stock and put it in a soup kettle with ½ pound ground raw chicken meat mixed with 2 unbeaten egg whites and 2 crushed eggshells. Bring to a boil, stirring slowly, until it reaches the boiling point. Simmer uncovered and undisturbed for 30 minutes. Strain and use as Method I, above.

If salt.is used, use sea salt and remember that when the stock is reduced it will become saltier.

CHICKEN CONSOMME
Cleared and Improved Chicken Stock

1 recipe cold chicken stock
1 onion, stuck with 2 cloves
1 small carrot, scrubbed and quartered
1 stalk celery with leaves
½ bay leaf
1 sprig thyme
2 sprigs parsley
1 tablespoon tarragon vinegar
1 teaspoon lemon juice
½ pound ground beef
1 egg white with 1 crushed eggshell

Lift fat from top of cold chicken stock and simmer, uncovered, until it is reduced to half. Set it aside to cool. Add onion, carrot, celery, bay leaf, herbs, and vinegar. Stir beef with 1 tablespoon cold water and add it to the stock, along with the egg white and shell. Set the stock over heat and bring it to a boil, stirring constantly. When it reaches the boiling point, reduce heat and simmer uncovered and undisturbed for 30 minutes. Strain the consommé through a triple cheesecloth wrung out in cold water and laid across a sieve. Chill the consommé and serve as recipes suggest, or use it as a basis for strong and healthful soups.

BROWN STOCK OR BOUILLON

2 pounds shin or brisket of beef
3 pounds knuckle of veal, cracked
7 quarts fresh cold water
2 onions, stuck with 2 cloves
2 celery stalks
2 carrots, scrubbed and quartered
1 turnip, peeled and quartered
7 bruised peppercorns
2 bay leaves
1 sprig thyme
6 sprigs parsley
Sea salt to taste, optional

Sear the beef and bones in their own fat in a dutch oven or large kettle until they are well browned on all sides. Cover with the cold water and set aside for 1 hour. Bring slowly to a boil and skim off the scum. Add vegetables and herbs and bring back to a boil. Skim off scum again and simmer for 6 hours, skimming occasionally. Take from heat, strain through a cloth wrung out in cold water. Cool and chill the stock, lift off the fat, and use the stock for soups, casseroles, or sauces.

TO CLARIFY BEEF STOCK

1 onion, quartered
1 small leek, white part only
1 carrot, scrubbed and quartered
1 stalk celery with leaves
1 bay leaf
3 sprigs parsley
4 black peppercorns, optional
1 egg white and 1 crushed eggshell
1 tablespoon vinegar
½ tablespoon lemon juice
½ pound ground beef mixed with 1 tablespoon cold water
3 quarts cold beef stock or brown stock

Combine and mix all ingredients except the stock in a clean kettle. Lift fat off the cold stock and pour stock over the vegetables and meat. Set over medium heat and bring slowly to a boil, whisking constantly. Reduce heat and simmer uncovered and undisturbed for about 25 minutes. Strain through a triple cheesecloth wrung out in cold water and laid across a sieve. Store in a covered container in refrigerator up to 2 weeks. Use for clear soups and aspics.

Clear Soups

After clearing soups of fat, straining, and clarifying them, we usually add something else. The simplest additions are the most healthful, namely an envelope of plain gelatin or an egg. Stock with gelatin makes an extremely good diet lunch with a slice of sprouted-wheat bread and fruit.

BOUILLON WITH GELATIN
For One

1 ¼ cups strong beef stock   1 envelope plain gelatin
    or bouillon   1 teaspoon chopped parsley

Soften gelatin in ¼ cup of the cold stock for 10 minutes. Bring remaining stock or bouillon to a boil, take from heat, and stir in the gelatin until it is dissolved. Sprinkle with parsley and serve.

BOUILLON WITH EGG

1 cup clarified stock or   1 poached or six-minute egg
    beef consommé   ½ teaspoon minced parsley

Bring consommé to a boil, reduce heat to simmer. Meanwhile poach or boil the egg. Trim the poached egg or peel the six-minute egg carefully. Pour the soup into a wide cup and lower the egg into it with a slotted spoon. Sprinkle with parsley and serve.

ADDITIONS TO CLEAR SOUPS

Tomato juice. Add 2 cups tomato juice to 4 cups clarified beef consommé. Add 3 peeled, seeded, and chopped tomatoes. Sprinkle with 2 tablespoons chopped parsley.

Parmesan cheese. Sprinkle hot beef consommé generously with grated cheese.

Consommé gratinée. Toast slices of whole-wheat bread, spread them with butter, and sprinkle them heavily with grated cheese. Put soup in heat-proof cups, top with one or two pieces of toast, and push under the broiler until the cheese browns.

Vegetables. Cook thin-sliced carrots and celery, green peas, and green beans cut across into ½-inch lengths in water until partially done, and add vegetables to the soup before it is served. Asparagus spears or cauliflower roses may be used instead of the other mixed vegetables.

MILLE FANTI

1½ cups stale whole-wheat breadcrumbs
6 tablespoons butter
6 cups chicken broth
3 tablespoons chopped parsley
Grated Parmesan cheese

Place crumbs and butter in a deep, heavy pan in a 375° F. oven. Stir frequently until the crumbs are evenly browned to a rich color. Take from oven, add the broth, and simmer for 10 minutes. Serve sprinkled with parsley and pass the cheese separately.

Clear Vegetable Soups

"VEGE-BASE" SOUP

"Vege-base" is a blend of vegetables, soy beans, dehydrated vegetables, and herbal seasonings. It can be purchased at most specialty stores and health-food stores or by mail order, see page 248. Stir 1 rounded teaspoon of "Vege-base" into 1 cup boiling water.

WHITE VEGETABLE STOCK

2 quarts fresh cold water
2 carrots, scraped and
  sliced
2 onions, sliced
1 turnip, sliced
2 leeks, white part only,
  sliced

2 celery stalks, sliced
2 sprigs parsley
1 sprig thyme
1 bay leaf
1 blade mace
1 clove
4 peppercorns, optional

Sea salt to taste, optional

Place all ingredients in a soup kettle. Bring to a boil, reduce heat, and simmer for 45 minutes. Strain the stock, and if it is to be served with vegetables, add freshly cooked hot vegetables to the heated soup. Do not simmer the stock longer than 45 minutes or the good flavors will be lost.

Note: always retain the water in which vegetables were steamed and add it to soups or to vegetable stocks.

BROWN VEGETABLE STOCK

Heat 6 tablespoons butter in a heavy kettle, add the vegetables as for White Vegetable Stock, and toss or shake them in the butter until they are light browned. Drain off the remaining butter, add the 2 quarts fresh cold water, boil, and simmer for not more than 45 minutes.

POTATO SOUP

6 large potatoes, scrubbed
2 onions, sliced
2 sprigs fresh marjoram
  or 2 teaspoons dried
3 sprigs parsley
1 carrot, scraped and sliced

Sea salt to taste, optional
1½ quarts water, vegetable
  water, or water
  in which half a bunch
  of parsley has been
  boiled

2 cups scalded milk, or to taste

Put all ingredients except milk into a heavy kettle and simmer for 30 minutes. Take out the potatoes with a slotted spoon, draw off the skins, quarter the potatoes, and return them to the kettle. Continue to boil until all the vegetables are very soft. Put them through a sieve or blender—in batches—and blend into a smooth puree. Thin the soup with scalded milk to taste, heat to just under boiling, and serve with fried whole-wheat-bread croutons.

MARMITE
The Meal in Itself

1 pound boiling beef or
   brisket in 1 piece
1 2-pound chicken, dis-
   jointed, including neck,
   wing tips, and giblets
½ cup butter
1 blanched veal bone or 1
   soup bone
2 carrots, quartered
2 onions, sliced

2 turnips, sliced
3 leeks, trimmed and sliced
4 celery stalks
1 small white cabbage,
   trimmed and quartered
Sea salt to taste, optional
4 peppercorns
6 slices buttered whole-wheat
   bread
Grated Parmesan cheese

Sear beef in a large Marmite, earthenware casserole, or heavy kettle. Brown the chicken in a pan in half the butter and add it with bones to the kettle. Add 6 quarts fresh cold water. Brown all vegetables except cabbage in the pan with the remaining ¼ cup butter and add to the kettle. Cover and simmer for 1½ hours. Take out meat and vegetables, set them aside, and simmer the stock for 4 hours, skimming frequently. In the meantime put up the cabbage in cold water to cover and cook it until tender. Let it cool in its broth. Put all vegetables and meat in the kettle and heat to boiling. Prepare slices of whole-wheat toast with cheese as for Onion Soup, page 116, and brown them under the broiler or in the oven. Serve the soup in wide plates or earthenware bowls with vegetables, beef, and chicken in each plate and the browned bread on top. Pass grated Parmesan cheese.

LEEK AND POTATO SOUP

1 bunch leeks	3 large potatoes, scrubbed
⅓ cup butter	Sea salt to taste, optional
1 large onion, sliced	2 cups scalded milk, or to taste

Trim, clean, and slice leeks. Discard the deep green ends but do include a little of the pale green that lies above the white. Melt butter in a large kettle, but do not let it brown. Add leeks and onion and cook covered over very low heat. Stir at intervals and do not let the vegetables brown. Meanwhile boil the potatoes in 1½ quarts water for about 20 minutes until tender. Take them out, draw off their skins and slice them roughly into the leek and onion mixture. Add the potato water, stir well, and continue to cook potatoes, leeks, and onion together until the leeks are very soft. Press the soup through a sieve or puree it in three batches through the blender. Thin the soup with milk to taste; it should remain a thick soup. Reheat and serve with toasted whole-wheat-bread croutons, crumbled crisp bacon, and/or chopped parsley.

ONION SOUP

¼ cup butter	Freshly ground black pepper,
4 large onions, finely	optional
sliced and separated into	6 thick slices whole-grain
rings	bread, cut into rounds
1 tablespoon brown mus-	with a large cookie
tard	cutter
2 quarts beef stock	4 tablespoons butter
Sea salt to taste,	4 tablespoons grated
optional	Parmesan or Swiss cheese

Melt butter in a soup kettle or earthenware casserole and cook the onions in it, stirring gently until lightly browned. Stir in the mustard and the stock slowly. Add salt and pepper, cook covered for about 20 minutes. Toast the bread rounds, butter them, and sprinkle with cheese. Put the soup into earthenware bowls and float a bread slice on each. Push them under a hot broiler long enough to brown the cheese, leaving the oven door open. Serve at once.

RED ONION SOUP

4 large red onions, thinly sliced
4 tablespoons olive or safflower oil
1 garlic clove, crushed
¼ cup finely diced green pepper
¼ cup roughly chopped walnuts

2 tablespoons chopped parsley
1½ quarts beef stock
Sea salt to taste, optional
Freshly grated black pepper, to taste
2 cups crisply fried whole-wheat bread croutons

Simmer onions in the oil in a large kettle, stirring slowly, until they are golden. Add garlic, pepper, nuts, parsley, stock, salt, and pepper and simmer the soup, covered, for 25 minutes. Serve in earthenware bowls with a heavy topping of croutons.

Creamed Vegetable Soups

Thanks to the blender, smooth, thick vegetable soups can be made without flour, rice, or any thickening agents. Cook vegetables in water or stock or sauté them lightly in butter before liquid is added. Add scalded milk or cream to the soup and blend into a smooth puree. In the summer, chilled cream can be added after the soup is cold.

BLENDER CREAM OF SPINACH SOUP

2 packages washed fresh
   spinach, or 1 pound
4 sprigs parsley, stems
   removed
1 onion, sliced and roughly
   chopped

2 cups chicken stock
1 cup heavy cream, scalded
Sea salt to taste, optional
3 hard-cooked eggs, sliced or
   riced

Wash spinach and remove wilted leaves and coarse stems. Place in a kettle that will just hold it, and shake it over medium heat. Do not add liquid. The water that clings to the leaves is enough to cook it. As soon as the spinach is wilted at the bottom of the kettle it is done (about 5 minutes). Drain well and retain the spinach water. Put spinach through the blender in two batches, adding the onion and parsley and enough of the stock to facilitate blending. Blend until smooth. Add remaining stock and cream, and thin with the spinach water. Spinach is high in sodium so little or no sea salt will be needed. Heat to boiling or chill and serve topped with the hard-cooked eggs.

OTHER BLENDER VEGETABLE SOUPS

Vary Blender Cream of Spinach Soup as follows:

Cauliflower. Steam 1 head cauliflower and break into flowerets. Blend with stock and cauliflower water, add cream, and serve hot or cold with a topping of toasted whole-wheat-bread croutons and snipped dill or chopped parsley.

Peas. Steam 2½ cups fresh peas in very little water until soft. Add stock and blend to a smooth puree, add cream. Serve cold with fresh tomato slices and chopped green mint. Or serve hot with whole-wheat-bread croutons and finely chopped scallions and parsley.

Cucumbers. As cucumbers are watery, it is necessary to dice at least 3 large or 5 small cucumbers. Peel only those parts of the cucumbers that are coarse and trim off the ends. Sauté cucumbers lightly in butter with 1 diced onion. Add chicken stock and cook until vegetables are very tender. Put mixture through blender with a teaspoon of snipped dill and sea salt to taste. Chill and fold in 1 cup heavy cream that has been whipped just long enough to thicken slightly. Serve cold with more snipped dill, or with finely cut chives and slivered scalded almonds.

Lima beans. Cook 1 cup baby lima beans and 1 medium sliced onion in 2 cups chicken stock until soft. Put vegetables and stock through the blender in two batches until smooth. Add scalded milk or more stock to taste and serve hot with crumbled bacon or cold, well-chopped summer savory.

Asparagus. Substitute 1½ cups steamed asparagus spears, cut across into 1-inch slices, for the lima beans. Garnish hot puree with browned whole-wheat-bread croutons; when it is served cold, garnish with riced hard-cooked eggs.

Cold Soups

ICED APPLE SOUP

2 pounds unpeeled greenings or cooking apples, sliced
1½ quarts fresh cold water
Slivered rind of 1 lemon
1 cinnamon stick
¼ cup brown sugar, or to taste

1 cup sweet cider
½ cup heavy cream, whipped
3 slices stale pumpernickel bread, blended or crushed to crumbs

Boil apples in a kettle with water, lemon rind, and cinnamon stick until very soft. Take out cinnamon stick and put the contents of the kettle through the blender in 2 batches until smooth. Sir in the sugar and cider and cook, stirring, until soup is reduced. Chill and serve with whipped cream sprinkled with crushed stale pumpernickel crumbs.

ICED CHERRY AND RED CURRANT SOUP

2 pounds red cherries,   ½ cinnamon stick
   pitted   2 cloves
1 pound red currants,   ½ cup brown sugar
   stemmed   2 cups beef consommé
½ lemon, sliced   1 cup medium cream
    ½ cup heavy cream, whipped

Put cherries into a pot with currants, lemon, and spices. Sprinkle with the sugar and set aside for 30 minutes. Add stock and bring to a boil. Reduce heat and simmer covered for 20 minutes. Pour the soup through a sieve and remove cinnamon and cloves. Blend until smooth and stir in the cream. Add as much of the broth in which the fruit cooked as needed to make 6 cups. Chill and serve topped with whipped cream and crisp whole-wheat-bread croutons. If the soup is too tart blend in brown sugar or honey to taste.

Dried Vegetable Soups

LENTIL SOUP

1 cup lentils, washed   1 small potato
1 ham bone, if available   3 cups scalded milk, or to
1 onion stuck with 2 cloves   taste
1 cup chopped celery   1½ cups fried whole-wheat-
   leaves   bread croutons
1 carrot, scrubbed and   2 tablespoons chopped
   diced   chervil

Soak lentils overnight in 3 cups fresh warm water. In the morning, pour lentils and their water into a kettle, add 1 quart heated water and the remaining ingredients, except the milk. Cover and bring to a boil, reduce heat and simmer. After ½ hour, take out the potato with a slotted spoon and draw off the skin. Slice the potato and return to soup. Simmer 1 hour longer, remove the ham bone and press the soup through a sieve or blend it to a smooth puree. Stir in the milk and season to taste with freshly ground black pepper. Serve in wide plates with fried whole-wheat-bread croutons and chopped chervil.

CREAM OF DRIED GREEN OR YELLOW PEAS

2 cups dried peas
2 onions, sliced
½ green pepper, seeded
  and sliced
1 bay leaf
2 sprigs parsley
2 sprigs thyme
2 cloves

4 peppercorns
1 ham bone, if available
1 cup milk, scalded
1 cup heavy cream,
  scalded
2 ⅓-inch-thick slices
  Bologna sausage, cut into
  ⅓-inch dice

2 tablespoons chopped parsley

Soak dried peas in a large kettle overnight in cold water to cover. Next morning, add 3 quarts water, vegetables, herbs, spices, and ham bone. Cover and bring to a boil. Reduce heat and simmer for 3 hours. Remove the ham bone and drain the soup through a sieve. Retain the liquid and put the contents of the sieve through the blender with the milk and cream, in 2 batches. If the soup is too thick, add some of the liquid that was drained from it. Return the puree to low heat and simmer, stirring, for 10 minutes. Serve garnished with Bologna sausage and parsley.

VEGETABLES

Cooked and raw vegetables are essential to daily healthful eating. If we are going to be serious about eating more healthfully—and not just stand there and talk about it—the first step is a new look at vegetables. We have fallen into the habit of dropping packages of frozen vegetables into small amounts of boiling water, and we forget that our great-grandparents, whose way of life we are trying to recapture, did not eat meat twice a day. The only nonfattening substitutes which we can seriously consider for our meat-heavy diets are vegetables—raw and cooked.

Prepared as they have been, we have turned them into simply an accompaniment to meat, rather than into an enjoyable part of dinner in their own right.

The following recipes are for luncheon and main dish vegetables. When the first spring vegetables are young and tender, they should be steamed according to the chart in this chapter, and served with butter. No one can improve on that.

When they are not in their first spring freshness, prepare them according to the following recipes.

OVEN-BAKED CELERY

3 medium heads fresh celery, preferably white

2 tablespoons butter

3 white onions, sliced across

2 cups stock, or enough to not quite cover

½ cup orange juice

1 tablespoon brown sugar

Remove coarse outside stalks from celery heads and trim the root. Cut them across into 6- to 7-inch lengths. Retain the tops and leaves for broth or soup. Split the heads down lengthwise in quarters, or into 5 or 6 sections if they are large. Arrange sections side by side in a well-buttered heat-proof dish and cover with the onion slices. Add stock and orange juice and sprinkle with brown sugar. Cover and bake at 375° F. for 50 minutes. Uncover, test with a fork for tenderness and continue to bake until most of the liquid has evaporated and the celery is tender.

BAKED ZUCCHINI

2 pounds young zucchini, sliced about ⅛ inch thick

2 small onions, sliced thin

2 tablespoons oil

1 pound tomatoes, peeled, seeded, and sliced

1 garlic clove, crushed

⅔ cup whole-wheat bread-crumbs

⅓ cup grated Parmesan cheese

2 tablespoons chopped parsley

Cook onion in the oil in a heavy pan until golden. Add tomatoes and garlic and cook until they are soft, about another 10 minutes. Add zucchini and stir gently over medium heat until the slices start to show a little transparency in the center. Transfer the mixture to a buttered heat-proof dish, sprinkle with crumbs and cheese, and bake at 400° F. until brown. Sprinkle with chopped parsley and serve.

RATATOUILLE
Baked Eggplant, Zucchini, and Tomatoes

1 one-pound eggplant,
   peeled and cubed
2 medium onions, sliced
   thin
2 garlic cloves, crushed
½ cup oil
1 pound young zucchini,
   cut across into ¼-inch
   slices

1 pound ripe tomatoes,
   peeled, seeded, and
   cubed
1 small green pepper,
   seeded and chopped
½ teaspoon each fresh
   minced thyme, basil, and
   oregano, or ¼ teaspoon
   dried

¼ cup chopped parsley

Sprinkle eggplant lightly with salt and set aside for 30 minutes. Rinse off salt and drain well. Cook onions and garlic in the oil in a wide pan until golden. Add eggplant and zucchini and stir very gently with a wood spoon until eggplant cubes are lightly browned. Add tomatoes, pepper, herbs, and half the parsley and simmer uncovered very gently for 50 minutes. Stir gently once or twice. Serve hot or cold, sprinkled with remaining parsley.

VEGETABLES IN FOIL

1 medium eggplant,
   peeled and cut into
   ½-inch slices
2 small zucchini, sliced
   ¼ inch thick
2 onions, thinly sliced
4 tomatoes, thickly sliced

2 sprigs basil or 1½ tea-
   spoons dried basil
1 teaspoon dried oregano
Freshly ground black pepper
3 tablespoons safflower oil
1 clove garlic, crushed

Trim eggplant slices evenly and arrange in the center of six 14-inch-long pieces of foil. Put a row of zucchini slices on the eggplant and onion slices on the zucchini. Top each package with 2 or 3 tomato slices. Lay 2 basil leaves on each tomato slice or sprinkle with dried basil. Add a pinch of dried oregano and a generous grinding of black pepper. Combine oil and garlic and pour ½ tablespoon over each package. Close them with a drugstore fold and bake at 375° F. for 25 minutes. Serve the packages unopened.

ASPARAGUS POLONAISE

2 pounds asparagus
⅔ cup butter
1 cup whole-wheat bread-
crumbs

2 hard-cooked eggs, yolk and
white riced separately
3 tablespoons finely chopped
parsley

Trim asparagus stalks and steam as directed in Vegetable Steaming Chart until bright green and just tender, about 15 minutes. Drain well. Heat butter, stir in breadcrumbs, and fry until brown. Pour breadcrumbs and butter over the asparagus. First sprinkle the riced egg whites, then the yolks, and then parsley over the crumbs and serve.

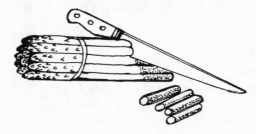

ASPARAGUS MILANAISE

2 pounds asparagus　　⅔ cup butter
1 cup grated Swiss cheese

Trim asparagus and steam it according to Vegetable Steaming Chart. Drain well. Melt 2 tablespoons of the butter in a pan and "tilt" asparagus in it until it is coated. Arrange asparagus on a heat-proof platter, sprinkling it with two thirds of the cheese. Brown the rest of the butter and pour it over the asparagus and sprinkle over the remaining cheese. Brown the cheese under a hot broiler with oven door open. Serve at once.

CORN PUDDING

3 cups fresh corn cut from   2 cups cream
   the cob   ½ teaspoon celery seed
4 eggs, separated   2 tablespoons melted butter

Cut corn kernels into a pudding dish. Scrape all the milk and seeds left on the cobs into the dish with the kernels. Beat egg yolks with cream and celery seed and add to the corn. Beat the egg whites until stiff and fold into the mixture. Sprinkle melted butter over the top and bake at 350° F. for about 40 minutes or until top is brown. If corn is not young and tender bake up to 1 hour, covering top loosely with a piece of foil.

HONEY-GLAZED CARROTS AND ONIONS

1 bunch very tender   3 tablespoons fresh orange
   young carrots,   juice
   scraped   3 tablespoons chopped
12 small white onions,   parsley
   peeled   3 tablespoons chopped
3 tablespoons butter   walnuts
3 tablespoons honey

Steam carrots with a little water until just tender, about 15 minutes depending on age. Boil onions in water until tender, about 15 minutes depending on size. Melt butter with honey and orange juice in a heavy oven-proof pan. Drain both vegetables well and "tilt" them in the pan until they are coated. Add enough water to come about half-way up the vegetables. Bake for 20 minutes in a 350° F. oven until all the liquid is absorbed. Shake them again to loosen and glaze all sides. Sprinkle with parsley and nuts before serving.

SQUASH WITH TOASTED ALMONDS

3 young acorn squash, cut
   in half and seeded
1 cup blanched almonds
2 cups whole-wheat
   breadcrumbs
¾ cup milk, heated

3 hard-cooked eggs, sliced
4 parsley sprigs
¾ cup grated Swiss cheese
2 egg yolks
Freshly ground black
   pepper

2 tablespoons butter

Parboil the squash in water for about 15 minutes, depending on age. Chop the almonds roughly in a chopping bowl.
Soak breadcrumbs in milk, press dry, and add to almonds in
bowl. Add eggs, parsley, and cheese and chop together to
mix. Bind the mixture with the egg yolks and season with
pepper. Fill the squash halves with the filling and arrange in
a buttered pan. Dot the filling with butter and bake at 375° F.
until the filling and the edges of the squash are lightly
browned.

SWEET POTATO CASSEROLE

5 sweet potatoes, cooked,
   skinned, and mashed
4 large apples, peeled,
   cored, and sliced
½ cup chopped pecans
¼ cup melted butter

¼ cup heavy cream
3 tablespoons brown sugar
¼ teaspoon each powdered
   cinnamon, cloves, and
   ginger
¼ cup raisins

Combine potatoes and apples with half the pecans, half the
butter, and all other ingredients in a buttered casserole.
Sprinkle remaining pecans and butter over the top and bake
at 375° F. for about 20 minutes or until top is browned.

BRAISED ENDIVE

Celery or leeks can be braised in the same way as the endive.

8 heads Belgian endive,   White pepper
  trimmed   1 cup homemade beef or
⅓ cup butter   chicken stock

Arrange the endive side by side in a heat-proof casserole. Dot each head with butter and pour over half the stock. Cover the casserole and bring the stock to a boil over high heat. Reduce the heat and barely simmer for about 15 minutes until the stock is almost evaporated. Turn the endive carefully and add the remaining stock. Cover again and simmer 20 minutes longer or until endive is tender. Remove from heat and take out the endive. Stir the remaining butter into the juices left in the hot pan. Pour over the endive and serve hot.

EGGPLANT CASSEROLE I

1 large eggplant, peeled   ¼ cup butter
  and cut into cubes   ½ teaspoon each chopped
2 onions, chopped   basil and thyme
1 cup thinly sliced celery   1 cup vegetable, chicken, or
2 young zucchini, sliced   beef broth
  ¼ inch thick   1 cup whole-wheat bread-
½ cup diced green pepper   crumbs
1 pimento, diced   2 eggs
2 tomatoes, peeled,   Freshly ground black
  seeded, and diced   pepper
       3 tablespoons chopped parsley

Melt butter in a heavy casserole and fry the onion and celery until they are transparent and tender. Add the vegetables, herbs, and half the broth and cover the casserole closely. Braise the vegetables over low heat for 15 minutes. Soak the breadcrumbs in the remaining broth, add the beaten eggs, pepper, and parsley. Stir the mixture into the casserole and bake covered at 325° F. for 15 minutes. Uncover and bake 15 minutes longer.

EGGPLANT CASSEROLE II

1 large eggplant, peeled
   and diced
3 large onions, chopped
6 large tomatoes
¼ cup olive oil
2 garlic cloves, crushed

3 sprigs fresh basil, chopped
3 sprigs fresh parsley,
   chopped
1 sprig fresh thyme,
   chopped
½ teaspoon paprika
Freshly ground pepper

Heat oil in a heavy casserole and add garlic. Add the onions and stir with a wooden spoon until they are puffed and transparent. Cut the tomatoes into the casserole, catching all their juices, and stir in the herbs and seasonings. Cook for 10 minutes, stirring. Stir in the eggplant, reduce heat, cover, and simmer until tender, about 30 minutes. If too moist, depending on consistency of tomatoes, cook uncovered for the last 15 minutes. If too dry add fresh tomato juice. Serve at once or cool and chill and serve cold as a first course with whole-grain bread and fresh butter.

PROVINCIAL ONIONS

2 pounds smallest white
   onions, trimmed and
   peeled
¼ cup butter
¼ cup olive oil or vege-
   table oil
4 tomatoes, peeled, seeded,
   and chopped
½ cup white currants

½ cup apple cider or water
Freshly ground pepper
Pinch of paprika to taste
½ cup reduced Coulis, page
   131
½ garlic clove, crushed
2 tablespoons cut chives or
   chopped parsley

Soak currants in apple cider or water. Steam onions in very little water in a covered saucepan for 10 minutes. Drain well and "tilt" them in the heated butter and oil until they are glossy. Set over medium heat and shake them for about 3 minutes. Add the tomatoes and currants and season to taste. Reduce heat, add Coulis and garlic, and cook, shaking, about 5 minutes longer. Sprinkle with parsley and serve hot.

ONION SOUFFLE

4 large onions, quartered	4 tablespoons butter
Freshly ground black pepper	4 tablespoons unbleached white flour
Less than a pinch of nutmeg	1/3 cup heavy cream
2 tablespoons chopped parsley	3 eggs, separated

Steam the onions in a tightly covered saucepan in one-half inch of water until they are soft. Drain them well, set the water in which they cooked aside, and chop the onions. Season with pepper and nutmeg and stir in the parsley. Melt the butter in the top of a double boiler over simmering water and stir in the unbleached flour. Gradually stir in 2/3 cup of the onion water and the heavy cream. Stir the sauce until it is smooth and thickened. Take from the heat and stir in the onions and the beaten egg yolks. Fold in the stiffly beaten egg whites and pour the mixture into a buttered soufflé pan. Bake it at once at 375° F. for about 35 minutes, or until puffed and brown and still soft inside. For a drier soufflé, make 45 minutes. Serve at once with brown butter or with tomato sauce.

BAKED ONIONS

7 large round onions, peeled and trimmed	Freshly ground black pepper
1/2 cup pecans	1 cup whole-wheat breadcrumbs
2 tablespoons chopped parsley	1/4 cup butter
2 tablespoons grated Parmesan cheese	

Cut tops off the onions and boil them with the tops in water to cover until centers are just loose enough to pull out, about 10 to 12 minutes. Remove the onions and reduce the water in which they were cooked to about 1 1/2 cups by boiling over high heat. Pull the centers out of the onions and arrange onions in a round buttered baking dish. Chop the centers and tops with the pecans. Add the parsley, and pepper to taste. Brown the breadcrumbs in the butter and mix half with the chopped onion. Refill onions with this mixture. Add the grated cheese to the second half of the breadcrumbs and spread over the tops. Add the reduced onion water to the pan and bake at 350° F. until crumbs are browned, about 30 minutes.

GREEK ONION CASSEROLE

3 pounds small white
  onions, peeled and
  trimmed
½ cup white currants
½ cup raisins

Strong beef stock to half
  cover
2 tablespoons brown sugar
1 tablespoon toasted wheat
  germ

½ cup heavy cream

Place onions, currants, and raisins in a deep casserole. Add stock to half cover and sprinkle with sugar and wheat germ. Cover the casserole tightly and bake at 325° F. for 1½ hours, stirring every 20 minutes and adding more stock if necessary. Add the cream and bake 30 minutes longer, stirring 2 or 3 times. Serve from the casserole.

TOMATO COULIS

To serve with celery or other vegetables and to use in place of tomato sauce.

8 large ripe tomatoes
½ cup olive or peanut oil
2 bay leaves
2 teaspoons minced fresh
  tarragon or 1 teaspoon
  dried

Freshly ground black
  pepper
1 garlic clove, crushed

Roughly chop the whole tomatoes in a chopping bowl and pour into a large heavy pan. Add the oil and bay leaves and stir until the tomatoes are completely wilted and soft. Rub them through a sieve or blend into a puree. Season with the pepper and garlic and chill the puree until needed.

COLD CELERY WITH COULIS

3 white celery hearts, cut   2 cups Coulis
6 inches long   ½ cup heavy cream
2 cups beef stock   2 tablespoons minced pars-
Juice and grated rind of   ley
1 lemon

Cut celery hearts in half lengthwise and arrange them side by side in a pan. Pour over the stock, lemon juice, and rind to just cover (depending on the size of the pan, more stock and lemon juice in the same proportions may be needed). Poach the celery gently until tender, about 15 to 20 minutes. Drain it well, arrange in a dish, and chill. Reduce the Coulis slightly by stirring it with the cream over low heat. Chill and pour it over the celery before serving. Sprinkle with chopped parsley.

BAKED SQUASH

6 young butternut or   1 cup dry whole-wheat
scallop squash   breadcrumbs
3 tablespoons butter   ⅔ cup grated cheese
Freshly ground black
pepper

Steam the whole squash for 15 minutes in a little water in a covered kettle. Cut off the tops and scoop out most of the meat and the seeds in the center with a melon ball cutter. Leave enough meat in the shells so that they are firm. Sauté the meat lightly in butter, season it with pepper to taste, and add the breadcrumbs. Stir for about 3 minutes. Take from heat, combine the mixture with half the cheese, and put it back into the shells. Butter the outside of the shells lightly and place them in a baking dish. Sprinkle the remaining cheese over the squash and dot with butter. Cover with a lid or with foil and bake at 350° F. for 20 minutes. Uncover the pan and bake 10 minutes longer. If a browner top is wanted, push the pan under the broiler for a minute with the oven door open.

DUCHESSE POTATOES

3 pounds potatoes   White pepper and the small-
6 tablespoons butter   est pinch of nutmeg
                      3 egg yolks

Steam the unpeeled potatoes until soft, about 25 minutes.
Pour off the water and shake them, covered, over low heat to
dry them out well. Draw off the skins and rice the potatoes
into a wide pan. Beat in the butter. Place pan over very low
heat and stir the potatoes with a wooden spoon until they are
very dry. Take from heat, cool slightly, and beat in the yolks.
The mixture should be piped or shaped, as the recipes require,
and browned under the broiler. It may be brushed lightly
with beaten egg before browning.

Pipe a circle of Duchesse Potatoes around the edge of any
vegetable that is going to be sprinkled with cheese and butter
and browned before serving. Asparagus spears, green beans,
cauliflower, or broccoli are suitable. Put cooked vegetables in
a shallow, heat-proof dish. Fill a pastry bag with the potato
mixture and pipe it, through a large, fluted tube, around the
edge of the dish. Sprinkle the vegetable with grated cheese
and melted butter and brown under the broiler, keeping the
oven door open.

APPLES AND SWEET POTATOES

3 cups mashed sweet   ½ cup brown sugar
   potatoes   ¼ cup chopped pecans
2 cups sliced apples   2 tablespoons butter

Spread a layer of sweet potatoes in a small buttered baking
dish. Cover with a layer of apple slices and sprinkle with
sugar. Continue with two more layers of sweet potatoes, apples, and sugar, ending with the apple slices. Sprinkle top with
sugar and pecans. Dot with butter and bake at 350° F. until
bubbling and browned on the top, about 40 minutes.

STEAMED SPINACH

1 to 2 pounds fresh spinach

Break off coarse stems and pick over the spinach carefully. Wash it in water six times. Put it into a deep saucepan or a small kettle that will just hold it and cover the pan or kettle tightly. Do not add water to the pan. The water that clings to the leaves when they are washed is sufficient to cook them. Cook over medium heat and shake pan several times. Just as soon as the spinach has wilted down to the bottom of the pan and is bright green it is finished. Drain and serve or use as directed. If salt is necessary, sprinkle ½ teaspoon sea salt over the spinach leaves in the saucepan before covering it.

Serve as is with butter, fried whole-wheat-bread croutons, with sliced hard-cooked eggs, or wherever cooked spinach is required.

MUSHROOMS WITH BROWN RICE

½ pound smallest mush-
rooms
½ cup butter
1 tablespoon lemon juice
1 onion, chopped
¾ cup brown rice

2½ cups strong beef stock
1 bay leaf
½ cinnamon stick
½ cup slivered, scalded
almonds

Clean the mushrooms with a damp cloth and trim the stems. Steam in a little water with lemon juice and 1 tablespoon of the butter. Set aside. Sauté the onion in the remaining butter until it is transparent but not brown. Stir in the rice and continue to stir over medium heat until it is glossy and transparent. Add the stock, bay leaf, and cinnamon, cover the pan, and bake at 375° F. for 15 minutes. Stir well, add the drained mushrooms and the almonds, and bake 10 minutes longer. Take out the bay leaf and cinnamon stock. If the rice is just tender, serve at once; if it needs a little more liquid, add some of the water in which the mushrooms steamed. Bake the casserole only as long as it takes for the rice to be "al dente" or just before it is soft.

DRIED MUSHROOMS

Dried mushrooms are imported from France, Italy, Poland, and many other European countries. They are usually the Boletus Edulis, but there are Cantrelles, Morels, and others that cannot be found in our markets. When they are properly dried and cooked they are better in some recipes than fresh mushrooms. This is particularly true of soups and sauces that require a stronger flavor. Dried mushrooms can be substituted for fresh mushrooms in all dishes, except where they are served as a plain vegetable or in recipes that call for whole mushroom caps.

TO DRY MUSHROOMS

To prepare, slice perfect, unpeeled mushrooms thickly. Quarter small mushrooms and leave very small ones whole.

Method I. Spread them on heavy paper and put in a warm, dry, and airy place. Intense sunshine on a hot, dry day is ideal. Lacking that, place the paper on a baking sheet and put into a very slow oven, at the lowest temperature. Leave the oven door open and watch carefully until the mushroom slices are dry and *leathery*.

Method II. String the mushroom slices or whole small mushrooms on a thin string with a coarse needle. Since the mushrooms should not touch each other, it is customary to make a knot between each piece. It is much easier to string a child's bugle bead (not plastic) between the mushrooms. Hang the strings in a warm, dry, airy place. Do not hang them in the kitchen as there is too much steam and moisture. A dry attic with windows is good in hot weather.

Method III. Hang the mushrooms, on their string, in a slow oven with the oven door open to allow for ventilation. Heat has to be low to prevent mushrooms from charring or acquiring a bitter taste.

TO USE DRIED MUSHROOMS

Method I. Soak them in cold water for 30 minutes, then put them into warm water until they are puffed and softened.

Method II. Rinse in tepid water, then pour over water that has just stopped boiling and set them aside for 30 minutes.

BRUSSELS SPROUTS

1 quart small Brussels sprouts	⅓ cup butter
	½ cup strong stock
1 cup sliced mushrooms	½ tablespoon brown sugar

Steam Brussels sprouts in very little water in a covered kettle until barely tender, about 10 minutes. Sauté the mushrooms in half the butter until they are wilted. Add the sprouts and stir them until they are glossy, then add the stock and simmer over low heat until tender. Stir sugar into remaining butter in a heavy casserole, until it is brown. Add drained sprouts and mushrooms and tilt to mix well. Serve from the casserole.

BRUSSELS SPROUTS WITH SEEDLESS GRAPES

1 quart small Brussels sprouts	¾ cup stock
	4 tablespoons butter, lightly browned
1½ cups sweet seedless grapes	Slivered rind of ½ lemon

Steam Brussels sprouts in very little water in a covered kettle until tender, about 15 to 18 minutes. Drain them well. Heat the grapes slowly in the stock. When they are hot, drain and add them to the sprouts. Add the browned butter and slivered lemon rind and serve.

BROWN RICE WITH ALMONDS

2 cups unprocessed brown
   rice or long-grain rice
1 teaspoon saffron shreds
¼ cup cold stock
1 onion, finely chopped
1 garlic clove, crushed
½ cup butter

¼ scant teaspoon each
   ground cinnamon, cloves
   and allspice
4 cups boiling stock
½ cup currants
¾ cup scalded almonds,
   roughly chopped

Steep the saffron in the cold stock. Sauté onion and garlic in ¼ cup butter until the onion is transparent. Stir in the ground spices, add the rice, and stir until the grains are well coated with butter and translucent. Add the boiling stock and saffron. Cover pan and let the rice cook over low heat, without disturbing it, for 15 minutes. In a second pan, heat the remaining butter and stir in the currants and almonds. Test a kernel of the rice and continue to cook it until it is just tender but not soft, about 20 minutes in all. Take it from heat, stir in the currants and almonds and serve the rice immediately.

RICE-STUFFED TOMATOES

7 large evenly sized
   tomatoes
Freshly ground black
   pepper
¾ cup brown rice

¼ cup butter
½ cup chopped pecans
½ green pepper, seeded and
   diced

Cut a lid from each tomato and scoop out the pulp with a teaspoon. Pepper the interiors lightly and invert tomatoes on paper towels to drain. Bake the rice, covered with 2 cups boiling water with 1 tablespoon of the butter, at 350° F. for about 35 minutes, or until the water is absorbed. Sauté the pecans in the remaining butter, add the cooked rice and green pepper, and stir well. Fill the tomatoes with the rice mixture. Arrange them close together in a heat-proof serving dish and add ¼ inch of water. Cover the dish with foil and bake at 375° F. for about 20 minutes.

ZUCCHINI WITH WALNUTS

8 young zucchini, ends
trimmed and sliced ¼
inch thick
⅓ cup butter
⅓ cup chopped
walnuts

1 apple, peeled, cored, and
diced
Rind of 1 lemon, coarsely
grated
1 teaspoon chopped oregano
or 1 tablespoon parsley

Steam the zucchini in ½ inch water in a covered saucepan over moderate heat for 4 minutes. Drain well and swirl the slices in a casserole with butter, walnuts, and apple over moderate heat. Grind pepper over it to taste and sprinkle with lemon rind and oregano. Serve at once.

BAKED CAULIFLOWER

1 large cauliflower
4 tablespoons grated Par-
mesan cheese
¼ cup melted butter

1 hard-cooked egg, optional
1 tablespoon chopped
parsley

Trim and steam cauliflower in about 1½ inches of water until just tender, about 15 to 20 minutes depending on size. Drain it well and arrange it in a buttered heat-proof dish. Sprinkle it heavily with cheese and then with the butter and bake at 400° F. until golden. Put under the broiler for a few seconds if a browner top is wanted. Rice the white and then the yolk of egg over the top and sprinkle it with chopped parsley. Serve at once.

Steamed Vegetables

Many of the previous recipes are based on vegetables that can be found all year round. In winter, whenever markets are low on fresh vegetables, prepare the onion recipes, which will be much more healthful than a canned vegetable. In spring and summer, when fresh young vegetables are available, eat them raw or steam them according to the following directions. Add a little fresh butter at the last moment before serving and season them as lightly as possible. The steamed young vegetables need no addition, but for a change they can be served in any of the following ways.

Asparagus. With Maltaise or Hollandaise Sauce; with brown butter and riced hard-cooked eggs; with brown butter and whole-wheat breadcrumbs.

Green beans. With toasted shaved almonds and brown butter; with small white onions sliced and divided into rings; under a lot of chopped parsley and summer savory; under crumbled crisp bacon, finely chopped onion, and parsley.

Lima beans. With crumbled crisp bacon and minced summer savory.

Wax beans. With whole-wheat breadcrumbs, sautéed in butter.

Beets. With orange juice and grated orange rind; with finely cut fresh dill; under riced hard-cooked egg and finely chopped parsley.

Brussels sprouts. With crumbled cooked chestnuts.

Carrots. With fine brown sugar and chopped parsley.

Cauliflower. With Hollandaise Sauce and fresh cut dill; with a pinch of brown sugar and whole-wheat breadcrumbs browned in butter.

Spinach. Under riced hard-cooked eggs, chopped parsley, and fried whole-wheat croutons; with poached or six-minute eggs; with crumbled cooked chestnuts.

Squash. With minced summer herbs: chervil, chives, and borage.

Zucchini. With slivered lemon rind and chopped chervil and parsley.

Use young homegrown, organically grown, or fresh market vegetables and steam them in small quantities of fresh water in a tightly closed kettle. Never overcook them, and save the water in which they steamed from broth, soups, sauces, and wherever cooking liquids are required. Vegetables, especially celery, beets, and spinach, contain natural minerals and salt, and they should not be salted. If unsalted vegetables are too bland, use sea salt.

Steam asparagus upright in the lower section of a double boiler and invert the upper section over it.

The following rules hold good for all vegetable cooking:

1. Eat vegetables as soon as possible after they were picked.

2. Eat vegetables as near as possible to the place where they were picked.

3. Eat vegetables raw or steamed in a small quantity of liquid.

4. Cook all vegetables for the shortest possible time necessary to make them palatable.

5. Cook vegetables until they are very soft only when they will be served mashed or when they are to be pureed for a soup.

6. Do not use soda to keep the vegetables green. If they are fresh and young and not overcooked they will be a bright green.

The following times for steaming vegetables are only approximate. The age of the vegetable, the size of the pieces or slices, and the length of time since it was harvested all influence the cooking time.

Vegetable Steaming Chart

Artichokes	25–35 minutes
Asparagus	12–25 minutes
Beans: green, lima, and wax	15–30 minutes
Beets	30–60 minutes
Beet greens	5 minutes
Broccoli	15–20 minutes
Cabbage, white, shredded	15 minutes
Cabbage, red, shredded	10–15 minutes
Cauliflower	15–25 minutes
Celery, sliced	15–20 minutes
Corn	8–12 minutes
Eggplant, sliced	15–20 minutes
Kale	5 minutes
Kohlrabi, sliced	25 minutes
Okra, sliced	15–20 minutes
Onions	20–30 minutes
Parsnips	30–40 minutes
Peas	10–20 minutes
Potatoes, new	15 minutes
Potatoes, medium	20–30 minutes
Potatoes, sweet	30 minutes
Pumpkin, sliced	25–40 minutes
Rutabaga, diced	35–40 minutes
Spinach	4–5 minutes
Squash, summer, sliced	15–20 minutes
Squash, Hubbard, sliced	25–40 minutes
Swiss chard	15–20 minutes
Tomatoes	5–10 minutes
Turnips, sliced	20–30 minutes

Very young vegetables will take a little less time, old vegetables will need the maximum time.

FISH AND SHELLFISH

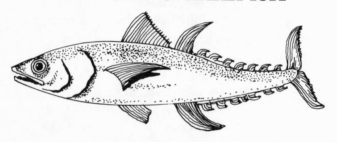

Fish and shellfish are important factors in healthful eating, and doubly so where weight is being watched. Because their flavor is naturally mild and bland, many recipes combine them with heavy sauces. Here they are put back into simpler concoctions—baked, poached, broiled, and baked in paper. Served hot or cold they are a prime source of protein, rich in vitamin A and the B-complex group, and low in calories. While we have sworn off canned and processed foods, quick-frozen fish is still recommended for anyone who does not live near the coast or in an area where fresh fish is available. It is freshly caught, cleaned, and immediately frozen.

Fish cooks in a short time, does not require complicated preparations, and is a relatively inexpensive food. When a gain in health means that weight has to be lost, it should be eaten at least four times a week.

With fish, as with meat, there is not as much need for

recipes as there is need for general advice and instruction in the basic methods of preparation. The fish dishes can be varied with light sauces, accompaniments, garnishes, or relishes, but basically fish is prepared in three healthful ways, and the variations fit around these simple processes.

The first rule for good and healthful fish cookery is—*do not overcook.*

To Broil Fish

Place fish on foil-covered broiler rack or pan, or into a broil-and-serve pan. Preheat broiler as high as it will go and place the rack or pan in such a way that the surface of the fish is as many inches from the source of heat as the recipes specify, or according to the following suggestions:

Fish fillets. From ¼ to 1 inch thick, should be broiled 2 inches from source of heat for 6 to 10 minutes, depending on thickness. They may be broiled more slowly when they are placed farther from the source of heat, as some of the recipes suggest. *Do not turn fillets.*

Fish steaks. From ½ to 1½ inches thick, should be broiled 2 inches from source of heat for 6 to 15 minutes, depending on thickness. Turn steaks once after about one third of the cooking time has elapsed, or after 2 to 5 minutes, depending on thickness.

Split fish. Place the fish, skin side down, 2 to 3 inches from source of heat and broil for 6 to 12 minutes, depending on thickness. *Do not turn.*

Whole dressed fish. Place a thin fish, such as flounder, 3 inches from source of heat and broil it for about 5 minutes on the first side. Turn it carefully and broil for 5 to 10 minutes on the second side, depending on thickness. Place a thicker fish, such as mackerel or bass, about 6 inches from source of heat and broil it for about the same length of time as the thinner fish, turning it in the same way.

Brush fish before broiling with any of the following mixtures. Baste it with the same mixture, and always brush it after it is turned. The quantities are for 6 servings of fish.

1. 3 tablespoons melted butter or oil, 1 tablespoon lemon juice.

2. 3 tablespoons melted butter or oil, 1½ tablespoons minced onion, ½ teaspoon minced thyme or oregano, 1 tablespoon lemon juice.

3. 3 tablespoons melted butter or oil, 1 tablespoon mild brown mustard, ½ tablespoon lemon juice, and ½ tablespoon cut dill.

4. 3 tablespoons melted butter or oil, 1 tablespoon lemon juice, grated rind of the lemon, and 2 teaspoons cut chives.

The most common of the fish suitable for broiling are:

Fillets	Steaks	Split	Dressed Whole
Bluefish	Cod	Bluefish	Bluefish
Cod	Halibut	Bonito	Butterfish
Flounder	Salmon	Mackerel	Flounder
Haddock	Swordfish	Mullet	Mackerel
Mackerel	Fresh tuna	Whitefish	Mullet
Mullet			Shad
Ocean perch			Smelts
Sea bass			Whitefish
Sole			

BROILED SHAD AND ROE

1 3-pound boned shad	2 tablespoons finely cut
2 shad roes	pimento
¼ cup melted butter	2 tablespoons finely chopped
1 tablespoon lemon juice	green pepper
Sea salt to taste, optional	1 tablespoon finely chopped
Freshly ground white	parsley
pepper	⅔ cup sour cream, whipped

Preheat broiler to maximum heat. Arrange shad skin side down on foil-covered rack or in foil pan. Put roes next to it and brush both with combined butter, lemon juice, and pepper. Broil shad 2 inches below the source of heat for about 4 minutes. Brush again with the butter and broil for about 5 more minutes. Mix pimento, green pepper, and parsley with the sour cream. Spread it thinly over the shad and broil 2 minutes longer. Serve with steamed potatoes and lemon wedges.

PORTUGUESE FISH STEAKS

6 fish steaks, 1 inch thick	½ cup thick mayonnaise
3 tablespoons melted	2 tablespoons minced onion
butter	2 tablespoons parsley
1 tablespoon lemon juice	2 tomatoes, peeled, seeded,
Freshly ground white	finely chopped, and
pepper	pressed dry
2 egg whites, beaten stiff	

Brush steaks with combined butter, lemon juice, and pepper. Broil 2 inches from the source of heat for about 3 minutes. Turn them carefully, brush again, and broil 4 minutes longer. Beat egg whites very stiff, fold in the mayonnaise, onion, parsley, and tomato and spread the mixture evenly on the 6 steaks. Broil 2 minutes longer with oven door open until tops are puffed and brown.

Note: ½ cup finely diced cucumber may be substituted for one tomato.

SALMON STEAKS

6 salmon steaks, 1 inch
thick
3 tablespoons melted
butter
1 tablespoon lemon juice
Freshly ground white
pepper
1 recipe Hollandaise Sauce

¼ cup minced sautéed mushrooms, all butter pressed
out
2 tablespoons minced herbs:
parsley, tarragon, chervil,
and chives, or just pars-
ley

Broil the steaks according to directions on page 143, brushing with a mixture of butter, lemon juice, and pepper. When
they are done, take out the rack and quickly spread each steak
with Hollandaise Sauce mixed with chopped mushrooms and
herbs. Push the rack back under the broiler and watch carefully as the surface of the sauce browns. Serve at once with
steamed potatoes.

BAKED FLOUNDER WITH HAZELNUT BUTTER

3 pounds flounder or sole
fillets
2 medium onions, sliced
thin
2 sprigs each, dill and
thyme
1 bay leaf
⅓ cup butter

¾ cup chopped hazelnuts or
filberts
1 onion, finely chopped
Juice and grated rind of 1
lemon
2 tablespoons chopped
parsley

If possible use parched hazelnuts. Wash off the salt and
chop them medium fine. Arrange the fillets on a bed of onion
slices in a buttered shallow heat-proof pan. Add the herbs and
bay leaf. Bake at 350° F. for 10 minutes. Meanwhile prepare
the sauce. Heat the butter, add nuts and chopped onion, and
fry until the onion is puffed and golden. Add the lemon juice,
rind, and 2 tablespoons water and pour the sauce over the
fillets in the oven. Bake about 15 minutes longer, depending
on the thickness of the fillets. As soon as they are opaque and
flake easily, serve them sprinkled with parsley.

BROILED FISH FILLETS

2 pounds sole, flounder,
scrod, haddock, pom-
pano, or whiting fillets,
or frozen fresh fillets
½ cup oil
1 recipe Hollandaise
Sauce

2 tomatoes, peeled, seeded,
and diced
2 tablespoons chopped fresh
basil, chervil, and parsley.
If not available use parsley
only.

Marinate fillets in oil for 20 minutes. Drain them well and arrange them in a foil-lined pan. Broil them 4 inches from a preheated broiler until they are golden, about 15 minutes. Do not turn. In the meantime prepare the Hollandaise Sauce, then fold in the tomato dice and herbs. Ladle a line of the sauce down the length of each fillet and return it to the hot broiler for a few seconds, or serve the sauce with the fillets.

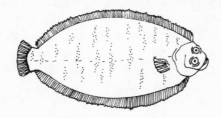

To Poach Fish

Fish are poached in a small quantity of liquid for a very short time. The liquid should come about half-way up the side of the piece of fish, whether it is a fillet, a steak, or a small whole fish. The fish should either be prepared in the same pan from which it will be served or it should be poached in a pan with a lid and then transferred to an open pan with a spatula or pancake turner. Poaching an average fillet, a drawn trout, or a one-inch-thick fish steak takes from 6 to 10 minutes. The fish is done when the meat is white and no longer transparent and can be flaked easily with a fork. If you are testing with a fork, test the *underside* of the fish.

POACHED FILLETS OF FISH VERONIQUE

2½ pounds sole, halibut, haddock, or flounder fillets
Sea salt to taste, optional
Freshly ground pepper to taste
2 tablespoons butter
1 large onion, minced
3 shallots or spring onions, minced
⅔ cup fish stock
1 teaspoon fresh lemon juice
½ cup heavy cream
1 egg yolk
3 cups stemmed green seedless grapes
⅓ cup heavy cream, whipped

Melt the butter in a heavy pan. Add the onion and shallots and arrange seasoned fish fillets close together on top of them. Add the fish stock and lemon juice and cover the pan with a piece of wax paper cut in a circle to fit the pan. Cut a small vent in the center of the paper and put the lid of the pan over the paper. Bring the fish to a boil and boil gently for about 8 minutes or until the meat of the fish is white and done. Remove lid and paper and transfer the fillets to a heat-proof serving pan. Keep them hot. Beat cream and egg yolk together, add to the liquids left in the pan, and stir over very low heat until thickened. Add the grapes and continue to stir until they are heated through. *Do not let the sauce come to a boil after the egg yolk is added.* Fold the whipped cream into the sauce and pour it over the fish fillets. Run the pan under a hot broiler long enough to lightly brown the cream. Keep the oven door open and watch carefully.

COLD STEAMED SALMON

1 darne or center cut of salmon, weighing 2½ to 3 pounds
1 bay leaf
4 peppercorns
Sea salt to taste, optional
1 onion, sliced
3 tomatoes, peeled and sliced
2 lemons, cut into wedges
2 hard-cooked eggs, sliced
Parsley sprigs
1 recipe Black Olive Sauce

Bring bay leaf, seasonings, and onion to a boil in 2 inches of water in a heavy kettle or dutch oven. Boil for 10 minutes. Place a trivet in the bottom so that the fish can be steamed above the boiling water. Wrap fish in cheesecloth and put it on the trivet. Cover kettle closely and steam the fish for about 1 minute per ounce or 40 minutes for a 2½-pound cut. Lift fish out carefully and let it cool before unwrapping it. When it is cold, unwrap and drain it well. Arrange the fish on a platter with a garnish of sliced tomatoes, lemon wedges, hard-cooked egg slices and parsley. Pass Black Olive Sauce separately (see page 176).

POACHED SALMON STEAKS WITH TOMATOES

6 one-inch-thick salmon
   steaks
Sea salt to taste, optional
Freshly ground pepper to
   taste
4 tablespoons butter
2 medium onions, minced
4 shallots, minced

1 small clove garlic, stuck
   with a wooden pick
1½ cups tomatoes, peeled,
   seeded, and chopped
¼ cup finely chopped
   parsley
½ cup fish stock
2 teaspoons lemon juice

1 recipe Hollandaise Sauce

Melt half the butter in a skillet and stir in the onions and shallots until they are transparent but not brown. Add the seasoned fish steaks and the garlic. Divide the tomatoes over the steaks and sprinkle them with chopped parsley. Add the fish stock and lemon juice and cover the pan with wax paper. Tear or cut a small hole in the paper and put the lid of the pan over the paper. Bring to a boil and boil for 10 minutes. Remove lid and paper and shake the pan to loosen the onions. Remove the garlic. Divide the remaining butter over the steaks and serve with Hollandaise Sauce.

POACHED FISH FILLETS

6 fish fillets   1 clove
1 small onion, sliced   ½ bay leaf
3 peppercorns   Sea salt to taste, optional
              1 recipe Butter and Nut Sauce

Bring onion, peppercorns, clove, and bay leaf to boiling point in 2 inches water in a heavy pan. Boil for 5 minutes, then reduce heat to bubbling. Lower the fish fillets into the water, increasing the heat so that the water just continues to bubble. Poach the fillets as you would poach eggs and take them out with a slotted spoon as soon as they are stiffened and white, about 8 to 10 minutes. Arrange them on a hot serving platter surrounded with new boiled potatoes and pour over the Butter and Nut Sauce (page 177).

To Bake Fish

Another healthful method of preparing fish fillets, steaks, or whole fish is baking. It is as easy as the other methods and takes only a little more time. Cod, flounder, haddock, mackerel, sole, and ocean perch fillets can be baked. Cod, haddock, halibut, salmon, swordfish, and tuna steaks can be baked as can whole striped bass, catfish, pompano, sea bass, bluefish, flounder, mackerel, shad, trout, and many others.

If possible the fish should be baked in the pan from which it will be served. Many recipes for baked fish call for stuffings or accompaniments that are baked in the pan with the fish. Others are baked on a bed of vegetables that prevents the fish from sticking and at the same time lends it flavor.

For baked fish fillets allow about 6 ounces per serving. For one-inch-thick steaks allow 8 ounces per serving.

Times for baking fish depend on its thickness and whether or not it is *whole* (with head on) or *dressed* (with head off).

Baking Times for Small Whole Fish

Fish	Thickness	Baking Time per Ounce
Bluefish	1½ inches	1½ minutes
Flounder	1 inch	2 minutes
Mackerel	2½ inches	2 minutes
Sea bass	1½ inches	1 minute 40 seconds

Baking Times for Small Dressed Fish

Bluefish	1½ inches	2 minutes
Flounder	1 inch	2 minutes
Mackerel	2½ inches	1 minute
Sea bass	1½ inches	2 minutes
Brook trout	¾ inch	1 minute

Baking Times for Large Whole Fish

Cod	2¾ inches	9 minutes
Haddock	3¼ inches	10 minutes
Halibut	2¾ inches	10 minutes
Salmon	2¼ inches	10 minutes
Sea trout	3½ inches	14 minutes
Striped bass	2½ inches	12 minutes

Baking Times for Large Dressed Fish

Cod	2¾ inches	12 minutes
Haddock	3¼ inches	14 minutes
Halibut	2¾ inches	11 minutes
Salmon	2¼ inches	11 minutes
Sea trout	3½ inches	15 minutes
Striped bass	2½ inches	16 minutes

BAKED DRESSED FISH

1 four-pound dressed bass, bluefish, shad, cod or haddock
2 tablespoons peanut oil
Sea salt to taste, optional
Freshly ground pepper to taste
4 to 5 medium tomatoes, peeled, seeded and diced
2 onions, thinly sliced and separated into rings
½ green pepper, seeded and finely sliced
1 pimento, cut into thin strips
2 teaspoons dried oregano
2 cups graham cracker crumbs
3 tablespoons melted butter
1 cup fish or vegetable stock
1 tablespoon butter
2 lemons, sliced
½ bunch fresh watercress

Rub fish with oil and season to taste. Put into a buttered baking dish and add the tomatoes and half the onion. Bake at 400° F. for 30 minutes, basting every 10 minutes. In the meantime, wilt the remaining onion, pepper, and pimento in the butter with the oregano. Add the cracker crumbs and stock and simmer until the fish is done. Spread the mixture over the fish, dot with butter, and bake 12 minutes longer until crumbs are lightly browned. Garnish the fish with lemon slices and watercress. If the slight sweetness in the cracker crumbs does not appeal, substitute whole-wheat breadcrumbs.

BAKED FISH FILLETS

(If frozen fillets are used, thaw them before cooking.)

2¼ pounds fish fillets
Sea salt to taste, optional
Freshly ground pepper to taste
6 tablespoons melted butter or peanut oil

1½ tablespoons fresh lemon juice
1 tablespoon minced onion
2 oranges, sliced
½ cup French Dressing
1½ tablespoons cut chives
¼ cup crumbled Bleu or Roquefort cheese

Season both sides of the fillets to taste. Dip them in a mixture of butter or oil, lemon juice, and onion. Arrange the fillets in a heat-proof baking dish and pour over any remaining butter mixture. Bake them at 350° F. for 25 to 30 minutes. In the meantime marinate the orange slices in the French Dressing. When fillets flake easily, serve them surrounded with the drained orange slices, with a sprinkling of chives on each orange slice.

BAKED FISH STEAKS

2½ to 3 pounds halibut steaks, cut 1-inch thick
6 slices bacon
½ cup light cream
1½ cups whole-wheat breadcrumbs

3 tablespoons melted butter
3 tablespoons chopped parsley
1 bunch cleaned watercress
1 pound green seedless grapes, divided into small bunches

Arrange the fish steaks in a shallow buttered baking dish. Top each steak with a slice of bacon and add the cream. Bake uncovered at 375° F. for 30 minutes or until steaks flake easily when tested with a fork. Take off the bacon slices and cover the fillets with a mixture of the breadcrumbs, butter, and parsley. Return the bacon and bake 10 to 12 minutes longer or until breadcrumbs are lightly browned. Serve with a garnish of watercress and green seedless grapes.

FISH FILLETS BAKED IN SOUR CREAM

2¼ pounds fish fillets
1 onion, thinly sliced
1 lemon, thinly sliced
Sea salt to taste, optional
Freshly ground pepper, to
    taste
1 cup sour cream,
    whipped

1½ tablespoons finely cut
    chives (or dill if it is
    available)
1 teaspoon mildest brown
    mustard
1 cucumber, scored and thinly
    sliced
¼ cup chopped walnuts

Lay fish fillets on onion and lemon slices in shallow baking dish, and season them to taste. Cover the dish and bake the fillets at 400° F. for about 30 minutes, or until fish flakes easily when tested with a fork. Whip the sour cream until light with chives (or dill) and mustard and spread over the fillets. Push the pan under a hot broiler until the surface of the cream is faintly browned. Serve surrounded by thinly sliced cucumbers sprinkled with walnuts.

COLD SHRIMP WITH MELON BALLS

1 pound shrimp, peeled
    and deveined
1 garlic clove, crushed
1 lemon, juice and grated
    rind
⅔ cup sunflower oil

¼ cup finely chopped
    parsley
¼ cup finely chopped
    onion
1½ cups cantaloupe melon
    balls
¼ cup chopped walnuts

Add shrimp to 3 cups rapidly boiling water. As soon as the water returns to a boil, time them to cook for just 4 minutes. Rinse shrimp under cold water for an instant, drain well, and immediately put them into a bowl with garlic, lemon juice and rind, oil, parsley, and onion. Marinate in the refrigerator for 30 minutes. Stir in the melon balls and serve with walnuts sprinkled over the top.

SKEWERED BROILED SHRIMP

2 pounds or about 36 medium shrimp, peeled and deveined
1 garlic clove, crushed
Juice and grated rind of 2 lemons

½ cup sunflower oil
¼ cup finely chopped parsley
2 teaspoons chopped fresh or crushed dried rosemary

¼ cup finely chopped onion

Marinate the shrimp with the other ingredients in the refrigerator for 1 hour, turning them several times. Shake off as much of the marinade as possible and string the shrimp on 6 small skewers. Go down through the center back of each shrimp and push them up against each other so they form a solid flat surface. Arrange skewers on a foil-lined broiler pan and divide the marinade over them. Spoon as much of the onion and herbs onto them as possible. Broil on the top shelf of the broiler for about 7 minutes until browned. Serve as they are, browned side up.

MEAT AND POULTRY

Meat and poultry are more than desirable on the menus of healthful eaters, *but in moderation*. If naturally fed meat can be obtained, all the better. Meat and poultry may be eaten in any quantity, always remembering that at least half the daily food should be fruit and vegetables. In meat and poultry, as in everything else, the simplest preparations are the best—which does not mean boiling, frying, or roasting meat until it is gray.

Naturally fed cattle reaches its absolute perfection in Japan, in the Kobe beef we have all heard about. This beef turns our beautiful steaks into shoe leather by comparison, and it is all done with careful feeding—and massage.

The steers are not really naturally fed except for their grazing land. Their pasturage is supplemented with rice and beans, or combined bran of rice and beans. They have a rubbing each day with a ginlike liquid to distribute their fat (although some say they are massaged with beer). As they grow older their diet is supplemented with beer fed from bottles. If additives could all be like that, we too could boast the healthiest and best beef in the world! The Japanese can afford his incomparable meat because he eats it in small quantities—cut paper thin for Sukiyaki or broiled on tiny individual grills at the table. They do not eat *pounds* of steak, but *ounces*.

Meat is the backbone of the average American family's diet and the richest single source we have for complete protein, iron, thiamine, and important vitamins. If it does not become practically the only food we eat (some American men have almost reached this extreme state) it is our greatest blessing. Eat all meats, liver, bacon, poultry, but no luncheon meats and not too much rich pork or ham. Serve meat with its own juices and sauces but not with gravies or condiments.

ROAST BEEF

The American Sunday dinner roast is at its best when it is simply prepared and roasted to the rare or medium stage. Preheat the oven to 325° F. Place meat in shallow, open roasting pan, fat side up. If a meat thermometer is used, insert it through the fat into the thickest part, without touching bone. Do not add any liquid to the pan. Roast beef uncovered without basting.

Weight of Roast	Roasting Time Rare	Roasting Time Medium
4 pounds	1¾ hours	2 hours
6 pounds	2¼ hours	2½ hours
8 pounds	3 hours	3½ hours

The meat thermometer will register 140° F. for rare, or 160° F. for medium.

Serve the beef with its natural juices, not with thickened gravy. If seasonings are wanted, sprinkle with sea salt and pepper before roasting.

FILET OF BEEF

The most beautiful and expensive of the beef roasts, filet should be larded or barded. Have the butcher lard it with strips of salt or larding pork or bard it with beef suet. The thin end is folded under and the filet is tied to hold its shape.

1 filet of tenderloin of beef	4 to 6 bacon strips
3 to 4 pounds	Sea salt to taste, optional
Freshly ground black pepper	

Lay filet on strips of bacon or pork in a shallow open roasting pan. Do not increase roasting time for a heavier filet. The time is based on *thickness*, and a heavier filet might be longer without being any thicker. Season to taste, brush with butter, and roast according to one of the following methods:

1. Roast in a 450° F. oven for 30 minutes for rare, 45 minutes for medium.

2. Brown the filet quickly on all sides in ¼ cup peanut oil. Roast it covered at 350° F. for about 35 to 40 minutes, basting frequently with the pan juices.

3. Roast at 325° F. for 18 minutes to the pound for rare, or for 22 minutes to the pound for medium rare. Never roast a filet until it is well done.

To serve a filet of beef, garnish the filet with watercress or parsley. Or serve the filet with its own juices or with Bearnaise Sauce or Quick Bearnaise Sauce. Accompany the filet with tomatoes filled with rice, with any of the steamed vegetables, with glazed chestnuts and with Duchesse or roasted potatoes.

FILET STEAKS

The French call the filet steaks by different names depending from which section of the filet they are cut. The *filet mignon* is a thick slice cut from the tail section of the filet. *Tournedos* are the slices cut from the heart of the filet. The *entrecote*, which means "between the ribs," is a slice of the *contrefilet* that we call a rib steak. A *chateaubriand* is the center piece of the filet. It is always prepared for two or more and sliced at an angle.

STEAK

Cooking steak does not require recipes as much as advice on purchasing and preparation for cooking. If you do not find the steak you want at your supermarket counter, ring the bell for the butcher and ask him to cut you a steak of the *grade, cut, and thickness* you prefer.

Some meat packers and retailers use brand names rather than grades to denote the quality of the meat, but the usual designations are as follows:

U.S.D.A. Prime is the top grade of meat, but it is not always available in supermarkets. It is the grade usually served in the best restaurants and hotels.

U.S.D.A. Choice is the best grade of meat that is usually available at the supermarket counters.

U.S.D.A. Good is the second best grade of meat available at all supermarket counters.

U.S.D.A. Standard and *U.S.D.A. Commercial* are rarely sold to the retail customer.

Tenderloin or filet, whole or in slices, is the tenderest and most expensive cut of beef. There are no bones or fat, and the filet requires larding or barding in order to prevent drying out. Larding means that lardoons or larding pork are inserted into the meat by means of a larding needle. For barding, slices of beef suet are placed over the entire filet and secured with string at 1-inch intervals.

Porterhouse and *T-bone steaks* include a T-shaped bone and a good portion of the tenderloin.

Sirloin steaks have a small portion of the tenderloin and a pin bone or double bone.

Club or *Delmonico steaks* include little or no bone or tenderloin.

Rib eye steaks are cut from the eye of the roast beef, trimmed from the bone.

Rib steaks are the same as rib eye steaks, including a portion of the rib bone.

Blade steaks and *arm steaks* are cut from the shoulder.

The thickness of the various steak cuts makes them suitable for different methods of preparation.

Steaks for broiling should be cut 1½ to 2 inches thick.

Steaks for pan broiling should be cut ¾ to 1½ inches thick.

Steaks for pan frying and quick cooking, as Minute Steaks and Steaks Diane, should be cut ½ to ¾ inch thick.

The tenderness of the meat cuts depends largely on the amount of work done by the animal's muscles and sinews while he ranged across the pasturage. The leg and shoulder cuts are never as tender as the loin or sirloin.

Meat sold by a retailer is usually fresh chilled, at a low temperature just above freezing. The meat becomes tenderer while it is stored at these even temperatures. However, the retailer sells his meat shortly after he receives it from the wholesaler. Some butchers select certain cuts and store them at proper temperatures for proper lengths of time in order to sell them (at higher prices) to the customers who are willing to pay for *aged beef*. Butchers will sometimes age meat on request, or sell it to the customer and then store it at proper temperatures. *Tenderness and flavor improve during this process but it cannot be done in the home refrigerator.*

Eat all meat as soon after it was purchased as possible. During the time that it must be kept in the refrigerator, store it uncovered or loosely wrapped in the coldest part of the refrigerator. Do not put it in the freezer compartment. If your refrigerator has a compartment marked for meat storage, avoid putting meat into it, unless it is the coldest part of the refrigerator and open on all sides to allow for air circulation. The meat should be as cold as possible without freezing, and air should circulate around it. Moist, tightly wrapped meats are less healthy and will spoil more quickly than a properly stored piece of meat.

Supermarket prepacked meats should be unpacked or the wrapper should be loosened *before* they are stored. Meat should not be stored in an overcrowded or closely packed refrigerator.

TO BROIL STEAK

Always take meat from refrigerator at least 1 hour before broiling. Remove the loose wrapper. Cut the fatty edge of the steak at intervals so that it will not curl or broil unevenly. Do not slash deeply into the meat or the juices will escape. Do not pierce the surface of the meat with a fork. Turn it with tongs or a spatula. Never use the prongs of a fork to handle steak. Brush steak with oil or melted butter, but do not season. Salt draws some of the juices out of the meat, and it consequently loses in food value and flavor. The broiler rack or grill need not be oiled, as raw meat does not stick to a very hot grill. Preheat broiler to red-hot or to as hot as possible. Place meat on hot rack or grill and place it under or over the source of heat so that the meat *surface* (not the rack) will be 2 inches from the source of heat. If meat has to be broiled more slowly, place it further from the source of heat but never reduce the heat of a broiler.

Broil the meat only long enough to change the color from raw red to lightest brown, about 2 minutes, to sear the surface and seal in the juices. Turn it with tongs, 2 spoons, or a spatula and broil the second side until the steak is brown and done. Serve it with this brown side up. Turn the steak only once.

The length of time that meat should be broiled depends on thickness and cut of the meat, on heat of the broiler, and on personal taste. A steak that is still rare feels soft and spongy, a well-done steak feels firm, and a medium steak feels semisoft. Press the steak with your fingers or be guided by the following suggestions until you are used to your own broiler. The most healthful steaks are quickly cooked and are eaten while they are juicy and not after they are overdone and dry.

Broil 1½- to 2-inch-thick steaks 2 inches from a red-hot source of heat for 12 to 14 minutes for rare, 15 to 18 minutes for medium, and 19 to 24 minutes for well-done. These times have to be adjusted if your broiler does not go to maximum heat, if the meat was cold, or if it was marinated or tenderized. Do not use commercial tenderizers. Season the steak, if you must, *after* it has been broiled. Serve it at once and do not carve it before it is going to be served. A large steak should be carved in such a way that the healthful juices can be spooned onto the meat.

TO PAN BROIL STEAK

The thinner steaks are suggested for pan broiling, but any steak that is over 1-inch thick can still be cooked on a *very hot broiler*. Pan broiling is preferable for the thinner steaks because it sears the surface evenly and quickly, making it possible to cook a rare thin steak. In other words, the greatest possible heat should be applied to the two surfaces of the meat in order to sear one of them and brown the second without producing a well-done steak.

Butter or oil a very hot, heavy skillet lightly, and quickly sear the steak on both sides. Turn the steak often with tongs or a spatula and pour off any fat that may accumulate in the pan.

A general rule is to pan broil a 1-inch-thick steak for 5 to

6 minutes for rare, 7 to 8 minutes for medium, and 9 to 10 inches for well-done.

Pan broil a 1-inch-thick *sirloin steak* for 6 to 7 minutes for rare, 8 to 10 minutes for medium, and 12 to 14 minutes for well-done.

Pan broil a ¾-inch-thick *rib steak* for 5 minutes for rare, 6 to 7 minutes for medium, and 8 to 9 minutes for well-done.

Pan broil a 1½- to 2-inch-thick *porterhouse* or *T-bone steak*, when a broiler is not available, for 7 to 9 minutes for rare, and 10 to 12 minutes for medium rare. The pan must be sizzling hot.

Pan broil a 1½-inch-thick slice of *tenderloin* or *filet mignon* for 6 minutes for rare and 7 to 9 minutes for medium rare to medium well-done.

Pan broil a 3- to 4-inch-thick *chateaubriand* for 16 to 20 minutes for rare to medium rare.

TO FRY STEAK

There are two methods of frying meat—in deep or shallow fat. There is no reason for deep-fat frying beef. Shallow-fat frying means that the fat covers the base of the pan and can extend half-way up the sides of the meat. This method is usually used for breaded veal, pork chops, or chicken. Shallow-fat frying is applied to beef only when chunks of meat are browned for stew or goulash or for beef olives or beef birds if the recipe requires.

STEAKS ALFREDO

6 slices beef tenderloin cut
  1-inch thick
3 tablespoons butter
2 small cloves garlic,
  crushed
¼ cup Tomato Coulis

6 tablespoons very heavy
  cream several days
  old
2 tablespoons minced herbs:
  parsley and chervil,
  tarragon and chives

Freshly ground black pepper

Have butcher split the 6 beef slices almost through, so that they can each be opened out to make a large, thin slice. Place them between two layers of wax paper and pound them to ¼-inch thickness. Heat butter in a skillet, add the steaks 2 at a time or more, depending on the size of the pan, and fry for about ½ minute. Turn the steaks and fry about 40 seconds longer for rare. Fry about 1½ to 2 minutes in all for well-done. Take steaks from pan and keep hot on a covered hot platter. Add Coulis and cream to pan and boil 2 minutes while scraping together the pan juices. Stir in herbs and pour the sauce over the steaks. Serve at once on very hot plates. This may be also cooked on an electric skillet at the table.

ACCOMPANIMENTS FOR STEAK

For healthful eating the meal should begin with fruit or a salad of fruit and/or vegetables. A vegetable course such as asparagus, broccoli, artichokes, or cauliflower may come before the meat. When the steak is served it may be accompanied by fresh watercress and Bearnaise Sauce. If there is no vegetable course before the meat, the steak may be accompanied by any steamed vegetable and steamed, Duchesse, or baked potatoes. Avoid French-fried potatoes, as deep-fat frying is not among the healthiest forms of preparation. Potatoes steamed in their jackets and swished through melted butter (to which chopped nuts, parsley, or even brown sugar has been added) are excellent with steaks, as are baked potatoes. Baked potatoes should be scrubbed before baking and may or may not be rubbed with butter. The skins should be eaten.

Sour cream and cut chives, fresh or melted butter, or parsley butter are good with baked potatoes. Try butter with shallots and parsley:

BUTTER SHALLOT SAUCE

½ cup butter   ¼ cup chopped shallots
                ¼ cup chopped parsley

Melt butter over low heat and do not let it brown. Add shallots and stir only long enough so that they are not raw, about 5 minutes. Add parsley and serve hot with baked potatoes.

This sauce may also be served with steaks that are not accompanied by baked potatoes. None of the highly spiced or hot sauces is healthful, nor do they contribute to the flavor of meat. Quickly cooked, flavorful, juicy meats should not be adulterated with highly seasoned sauces that take away from, rather than adding to, their goodness.

BRAISING BEEF

Braising beef is a more healthful preparation for the less tender cuts of beef than stewing it. Braising is actually a combination of steaming and baking after the meat has been quickly browned in fat or a combination of fat, oil, or butter. Braising is best done in a heavy, heat-proof casserole, dutch oven, or cast-iron kettle with a close-fitting lid. After being browned the meat is placed on a *mirepoix*, a bed of vegetables, with a very small quantity of liquid, and is braised until tender on top of the stove or in the oven. Sirloin tip, rump, round steak, blade pot roast, brisket, and oxtail are suitable for braising.

BRAISED BEEF

4 to 5 pounds beef, rump,   1 clove garlic, crushed
round, or blade pot   1 cup diced carrots
roast   1 cup diced celery
2 tablespoons beef fat or   ½ cup diced turnip
peanut oil   4 tomatoes, quartered
2 onions, sliced   1 bay leaf
¼ to ⅓ cup beef stock

Brown the meat quickly on all sides in the fat or oil in a
very heavy kettle over very high heat. Take out the meat,
reduce heat, and add the onions and garlic. Cook only long
enough to soften the onion. Add carrot, celery, and turnip
and stir 6 to 7 minutes longer. Add tomatoes, bay leaf, meat,
and ¼ cup stock. Cover tightly and simmer on top of the
stove until meat is tender, about 2 hours. Take out meat
and keep it hot. Press vegetables with braising liquids through
a sieve. Serve the meat with this sauce poured over it. If
necessary add a little stock during cooking.

LAMB WITH DRIED APRICOTS

3 pounds boneless lamb   1½ cups dried apricots
shoulder cut into large   1 tablespoon honey, or less
cubes   to taste
1 carrot, scraped and   ¼ cup shelled walnut meats
quartered   2 tablespoons chopped
2 medium onions, chopped   parsley
3 tablespoons oil

Make broth of lamb trimmings and carrot and reduce it
to 2 cups strained broth. Fry onions for 5 minutes in oil and
take them out with a slotted spoon. Brown the meat on all
sides in the oil, return the onions to the meat, add 1 cup broth,
and simmer covered for about 40 minutes. Add apricots and
honey and simmer covered another 40 minutes or until lamb
is tender, stirring often. Add more broth when necessary but
do not make it into a liquid stew. Add nuts and stir 5 minutes
longer or until they are heated. Sprinkle with parsley and
serve with brown rice.

CALF'S LIVER IN HERB SAUCE

6 ½-inch-thick slices of calf's liver
Sea salt, to taste, optional
Freshly ground black pepper
⅓ cup butter
1 small onion, finely chopped

Juice of ½ lemon
1 lemon, thinly sliced for garnish
2 tablespoons chopped parsley
1 tablespoon chopped chervil
2 teaspoons ground thyme
1 bay leaf

Season the liver slices and brown them quickly on both sides in half the butter in a shallow casserole. Always handle liver with a spoon or spatula. Take out the slices and keep them warm on a heated serving platter in a low oven. Add the remaining butter to the casserole and fry the onion in it until golden. Add the lemon juice, sprinkle with parsley, chervil, thyme, and the crumbled bay leaf and let boil up once. Pour the herb sauce over the liver slices and serve the liver with lemon slices, crisp bacon, and a tomato salad.

BROILED CALF'S LIVER STEAKS

3 pounds calf's liver, cut into six steaks, 1 to 1½ inches thick

6 tablespoons butter, melted
6 tablespoons peanut oil

Freshly ground black pepper to taste

Plan on about 8 ounces of liver per person. If the liver is tender, young, and properly cut, it will be well worth the expense. Brush liver steaks with the combined butter and oil and broil them under a hot broiler so that they brown quickly and remain pink inside. Depending on the thickness of the steaks this can take as little as 10 minutes on each side. Continue to brush with butter and oil and turn them as soon as they are brown. Season the steaks at once and serve them with quickly made Bearnaise Sauce.

VEAL CHOPS ON APPLESAUCE

Lemon Butter

½ cup butter, at room
  temperature
1 lemon, juice and grated
  rind

3 tablespoons minced parsley
Freshly ground black pepper
  to taste

Whip butter until creamy and light, stir in lemon juice to taste and all the rind. Add minced parsley and season with pepper to taste. Shape butter into an oblong on a piece of wax paper. Roll it into a short roll, by means of the paper, and chill or freeze it until needed.

Applesauce

6 large green apples,
  peeled and cored
1 long curl lemon peel

1 tablespoon brown sugar, or
  to taste

Peel apples in long strips that can be easily removed from pan. Slice apples into a pan and simmer them with 1 cup water, the apple peel, lemon peel, and sugar until they are very soft. Remove the peels and drain apples well. Sieve or blend them into a smooth puree. Spread on a hot serving dish, cover, and keep warm.

Veal Chops

6 loin or rib veal chops
¼ cup melted butter
Sea salt to taste, optional

Freshly ground black pepper
  to taste

Brush chops with butter, season to taste, and broil them under very high heat until brown, about 5 to 6 minutes on each side. Place them on the warm applesauce, put a round slice of icy lemon butter on each chop, and serve from the casserole.

VEAL CHOPS IN PACKAGES

6 veal chops, ¾ to 1 inch thick

Sea salt to taste, optional

6 tablespoons butter

¾ cup chopped green onions, or 2 onions, chopped

¼ garlic clove, crushed

⅓ pound mushrooms, chopped or sliced

1½ tablespoons lemon juice

½ cup stock (or if preferred, substitute ½ cup sour cream)

½ cup whole-wheat breadcrumbs

2 tablespoons chopped parsley

1 teaspoon chopped marjoram

1 teaspoon brown sugar

3 large tomatoes, peeled and sliced

Pound the chops lightly between 2 pieces of wax or butcher's paper and season to taste. Brown lightly in half the butter and take out of the pan. Add the rest of the butter and sauté green onions or onion and garlic for about 4 minutes. Add mushrooms and lemon juice and continue cooking until they are wilted and darkened. Stir in stock, breadcrumbs, herbs, and sugar and season to taste. Arrange the chops on 6 pieces of parchment paper or foil. Divide the mixture over them and cover with sliced tomatoes. Fold the chops into secure packages with a drugstore fold and bake them in a buttered baking pan at 375° F. for about 30 minutes. Serve immediately in the packages.

FRUIT-STUFFED PORK CHOPS

6 1-inch-thick pork chops
1 green apple, peeled,
  cored, and thinly
  sliced
6 dried prunes, pitted and
  chopped
¼ cup dried currants

1 lemon, slivered rind and
  juice
1 tablespoon brown sugar
Sea salt to taste, optional
Freshly grated black pepper
3 tablespoons butter
1 cup stock

Garnish

6 small greenings, upper
  half peeled and cored
¾ cup toasted whole-
  wheat breadcrumbs

¼ cup chopped scalded
  almonds
¼ cup thin honey
2 tablespoons butter

Have butcher cut a deep pocket into the fat side of the chops. Push in a few apple slices and prunes combined with currants, lemon rind and juice, a little sugar, and seasonings. Secure the opening with small skewers. Brown the chops lightly in butter in a heavy casserole, about 10 minutes on each side. Add stock, cover tightly, and bake at 375° F. for 45 minutes. For the garnish, fill the apples with a mixture of crumbs, almonds, and honey. Dot with butter and bake in ½ inch of water in a small pan in the same oven. Baste them several times. Serve the apples in the casserole with the chops.

HERBED CHICKEN IN CASSEROLE

2 broilers, quartered
4 sprigs fresh tarragon
2 sprigs fresh basil
4 sprigs rosemary
Sea salt to taste, optional
Freshly ground black
  pepper
3 tablespoons butter
3 tablespoons peanut oil

18 small white onions,
  trimmed and peeled
18 button mushrooms
1½ cups potato balls or ½-
  inch cubes
1½ cups chicken stock made
  from wing tips, necks, and
  giblets

Put up wing tips, necks, and giblets of the chicken in fresh water and bring them to a boil. Reduce heat and simmer to obtain 1 ½ cups broth for casserole.

Remove stems from herbs and push the largest leaves of each type of herb under the skin of the chicken pieces with a pointed knife. Mince the remaining herbs. Season chicken pieces with pepper and brown lightly in half the butter and oil in a large casserole. Turn to brown all sides evenly, then remove, and add the remaining butter and oil to the casserole. Add onions and mushrooms and sauté for about 7 minutes, then return chicken pieces to the casserole, cover closely, and reduce heat to simmer. After 15 minutes add minced herbs, potatoes, and strained broth. Cover and simmer about 10 minutes longer until potatoes are tender and stock is almost absorbed. This can be made with scalded dried herbs, but fresh herbs are very much better. To scald herbs, drop dried herbs into boiling water for a minute or two. Drain.

COLD CHICKEN WITH FILBERTS

2½ cups cooked chicken meat cut into large pieces	4 raw mushrooms, thinly sliced
1 white celery heart, scraped and finely diced	1 tablespoon lemon juice
	½ cup homemade mayonnaise
2 tablespoons finely chopped onion	2 tablespoons sour cream
	2 hard-cooked eggs, sliced
1 cup steamed baby lima beans	½ cup filberts or hazelnuts
	2 tablespoons chopped parsley

Combine chicken, celery, onion, beans, and mushrooms. Bind them with the lemon juice, mayonnaise, and sour cream beaten together. Arrange the mixture in a bowl and surround it with hard-cooked egg slices. Spread the filberts on a baking sheet and toast in a 400° F. oven for 12 minutes, shaking them every few minutes. Chop roughly and sprinkle over the chicken salad along with the parsley.

LEMON CHICKEN

2 small broilers,
quartered
¾ cup butter
½ pound button mush-
rooms, or large mush-
rooms sliced
2 large lemons, 1 sliced
thin, the other for the
grated rind and juice

½ clove garlic, crushed
Sea salt to taste, optional
Freshly ground black
pepper
2 tablespoons capers,
drained
2 tablespoons chopped
parsley

Melt butter in a wide, heavy casserole and stir in mushrooms until they are glossy and slightly darkened, about 5 minutes. Add lemon juice and rind, garlic, seasonings, and capers and bring to an even simmer. Add the chicken pieces, skin side down, and increase heat slightly until butter is bubbling again. Reduce heat again, put on a tightly fitting lid, and cook for about 15 minutes until the chicken pieces are browned, turn them over, cover again, and cook about 15 minutes longer. Cover chicken with lemon slices and parsley and serve from the casserole. If the capers are large they should be chopped.

BAKED APPLES TO SERVE WITH CHICKEN

6 large baking apples
Giblets of the chickens
¼ cup butter
1 onion, chopped

4 mushrooms, chopped
1 cup whole-wheat bread-
crumbs

Peel apples half-way down and core to within ½ inch of the bottom. Set chicken livers aside, cook giblets until tender, up to 1 hour depending on age. Retain broth. Melt 3 table-spoons of the butter, sauté onions and mushrooms about 6 minutes. Add the chicken livers and sauté about 4 minutes longer. Crush the livers, add crumbs and chopped giblets, moisten with a little of the broth, and fill the mixture into the apples. Set them in a pan, dot with the remaining butter, and add about ½ inch of broth. Bake them at 375° F., basting them a few times until they are soft, depending on the type of apple, about 35 minutes.

BROILER WITH SESAME SEEDS

2 large broiler,
  quartered
¼ cup peanut oil
¼ cup honey
¼ cup sesame seeds
¾ to 1 cup chicken stock
6 ripe peaches, peeled and
  cut in half

Brush the chicken pieces with peanut oil and bake in an open roasting pan, skin side up, at 350° F. for 10 minutes. Brush them again, add ¼ inch stock to the pan, and bake for 30 minutes longer, brushing and basting until they are golden. Push chicken pieces to one side and add the peach halves to the pan, cut side down. Brush chicken and peaches with the honey and sprinkle chicken generously with sesame seeds. Push the pan under the broiler and glaze the chicken for 1 minute. Repeat the honey brushing, add the last sesame seeds, and broil until the seeds are golden. Serve the chicken with the broiled peach halves and pan juices.

SAUCES

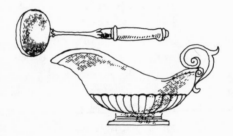

Sauces are healthy, with the exception of flour-thickened gravies, brown and white sauces, sweetened sauces, and all the highly spiced ones. There need be no sad farewells. Cream and yolks can thicken a sauce very satisfactorily, and the butters and egg sauces are not only good for us, they are desirable. Since all butters are made from pasteurized cream their benefits are lessened, but the unheated oils in mayonnaise and related sauces are needed in a healthy diet and even in a reducing diet.

Either yogurt and sour cream can be stirred into pan drippings to produce beautiful sauces, and they can be made smooth and beautiful more easily than the flour-thickened sauces. The great connoisseurs of good cookery have always been devotees of the mother sauces but they never acknowledged gravy. They have served meats either with their own natural juices, or with sauces that have nothing to do with what was left in the pan. The classic French Tournedos with Bearnaise is an example of an unrelated sauce, as is cold game with Cumberland Sauce, Salmon with Horseradish Cream, or Pheasant with Bread Sauce.

Dessert sauces can be made with honey, and a Sabayone Sauce made in this way is smoother than one made with sugar.

BLENDER BEARNAISE SAUCE

¼ cup tarragon vinegar
2 teaspoons minced tarragon
1 tablespoon minced parsley or chervil and parsley
1 tablespoon minced shallots

2 tablespoons fresh water
3 large egg yolks
1 tablespoon fresh lemon juice
Sea salt and black pepper to taste, optional
½ cup melted butter

At any time earlier in the day, reduce vinegar, herbs, shallots, and water to about 1 tablespoon. It will be practically a glaze, so be careful it does not scorch. Put yolks in blender with lemon juice and optional seasonings (use no salt if you are using salted butter) and run the blender long enough to break and smooth the yolks. Add the butter in a thin, uninterrupted stream with the blender running at highest speed. When the sauce is thickened, add the reduced vinegar and blend only long enough to mix completely.

VARIATIONS

1. Fold ¼ cup tomato puree into 1 recipe Bearnaise Sauce.

2. Stir 2 tablespoons cooked, chopped mushrooms and 1 peeled and chopped truffle into 1 recipe Bearnaise Sauce.

3. Fold ¼ cup steamed tomato dice and 1 tablespoon chopped parsley into 1 recipe Bearnaise Sauce.

HOLLANDAISE SAUCE

4 egg yolks   1 ¼ cups melted butter,
4 teaspoons cream   skimmed and warm
1 lemon, cut in half, pits removed

Stir the yolks and cream in the top of a double boiler until smooth and thick. Set them over a little simmering water in the lower section of the double boiler and stir in the butter, a little at a time, always stirring it in well before adding more. When the butter is incorporated and the sauce is smooth, finish it by squeezing in lemon juice to taste. If it shows signs of separating, stir in a little boiling water.

VARIATIONS

Sauce Fleurette. Fold ½ cup whipped cream into 1 recipe Hollandaise Sauce and add 2 tablespoons minced herbs: parsley, chives, chervil, or tarragon.

Sauce Maltaise. Substitute orange juice for lemon juice and fold in the grated rind of 1 orange.

Sauce Mousseline. Fold ½ cup whipped cream into 1 recipe Hollandaise Sauce.

Sauce Paloise. Fold 2 tablespoons finely chopped fresh mint leaves into 1 recipe Hollandaise Sauce just before serving.

BLACK OLIVE SAUCE

1 cup homemade mayon-   1 hard-cooked egg, white and
   naise   yolk riced separately
2 teaspoons minced tar-   2 large black olives, finely
   ragon   diced

Stir tarragon into the mayonnaise. Arrange it in a crystal bowl and sprinkle the surface first with egg white, then with egg yolk and finally with black olives. Stir the sauce before serving.

SAUCE REMOULADE

1 recipe mayonnaise
1 tablespoon mild brown
   mustard
2 teaspoons minced chervil
   leaves
1 teaspoon each, minced
   tarragon leaves and
   parsley

1 dill pickle, minced and all
   moisture pressed out
1 tablespoon minced capers
1 teaspoon minced onion
⅛ teaspoon anchovy paste

Fold all ingredients into the mayonnaise and chill. Serve with cold meats and shrimp cocktails.

WHOLE-WHEAT BREAD SAUCE

¾ cup milk
1 cup stock
1 cup fresh whole-wheat
   breadcrumbs

½ cup heavy cream
1 squeeze lemon juice
Freshly ground white pepper

Bring milk and stock to a boil and stir in the breadcrumbs. Reduce heat and let the sauce simmer for about 15 minutes. Take from heat and beat the sauce with a French wire whisk until smooth. Beat in the cream and lemon juice and add pepper to taste. Reheat the sauce in the top of a double boiler over boiling water. Season and serve.

BUTTER AND NUT SAUCE
For Fish Fillets or Vegetables

½ cup butter
¼ cup shaved or thinly cut
   shaved almonds, co-
   conut chips, or Brazil
   nut slices

1½ tablespoons fresh lemon
   juice

Melt the butter over low heat, stir in the nuts, and cook, stirring constantly, for about 4 minutes until they are lightly browned. Add the lemon juice and use at once. A little minced parsley may be added, to taste.

TOMATO SAUCE

3 pounds or 12 large ripe
tomatoes, peeled,
seeded, and chopped
6 tablespoons sunflower oil
2 tablespoons olive oil
Sea salt to taste, optional

Freshly ground white pep-
per, to taste
½ to 1 teaspoon brown sugar
1 clove garlic, crushed
3 tablespoons chopped
parsley

Heat oils in a casserole, add the tomatoes, and season to taste. Add sugar and garlic and simmer covered for 15 minutes. Add the parsley, stir well, and partially cover. Simmer about 20 minutes longer, stirring at intervals.

CUCUMBER SAUCE

2 solid cucumbers
Sea salt to taste, optional
Freshly ground white
pepper

¼ cup thick cream, preferably 2 or 3 days old

Peel cucumbers, cut in quarters lengthwise, and scrape away the seeds. Cut into short lengths. Drop into rapidly boiling water and boil for 5 minutes. Pour through a strainer and drop the drained cucumbers into a kettle of cold water. Drain *very well* and blend or sieve them into a puree. Try to squeeze as much liquid out of the puree as possible. Whip the cream, fold into the cucumbers, season, and serve very cold.

MINT SAUCE

¾ cup minced fresh mint
leaves
3 tablespoons brown sugar
or honey
¾ cup cider vinegar

⅓ cup fresh water
Sea salt to taste, optional
Freshly ground white pepper
to taste

Mix all the ingredients and stir until sugar or honey are dissolved. If preferred the sauce may be mixed in the blender until sugar or honey are dissolved. Then open the top and drop in the mint leaves and continue to blend until they are finely minced but not pulverized. Serve with roasted or broiled lamb.

MUSTARD SAUCE

2 tablespoons mild Dijon mustard
1 tablespoon lemon juice
Sea salt to taste, optional

Freshly ground white pepper, to taste
1 cup heavy cream

Beat mustard, lemon juice, and seasonings until smooth. Gradually beat in half the cream, little by little as for mayonnaise. Whip the remaining cream until very smooth but not stiff and stir it gently into the sauce.

LEMON SAUCE

1 large lemon, juice and grated rind
3 radishes, minced and pressed dry in a kitchen towel (cucumber may be substituted for the radishes)
1 8-ounce cream cheese at room temperature, riced

3 tablespoons minced fresh chives, parsley, chervil, or mixed herbs
Sea salt to taste, optional
Freshly ground white pepper
2 to 3 tablespoons sour cream

Beat lemon juice and rind with radishes and work in the cream cheese until smooth. Add herbs and seasonings and thin the sauce to taste with sour cream. Serve with zucchini, broccoli, or asparagus.

HORSERADISH SAUCE

½ cup freshly ground
  horseradish
½ tablespoon lemon juice

Sea salt to taste, optional
Freshly ground white pepper
1 cup heavy cream, whipped

Grate or grind horseradish just before folding it into the sauce. Serve at once.

HARD SAUCE

7 tablespoons butter at
  room temperature
1 cup honey

2 teaspoons lemon or orange
  juice
1 teaspoon grated lemon or
  orange rind

Cream the butter and beat in the honey, little by little, with the fruit juice and rind. Do not overbeat. Chill the sauce and serve it with hot puddings.

SABAYONE SAUCE

3 egg yolks
3 tablespoons honey
3 tablespoons Marsala

3 tablespoons finely grated
  orange rind

Beat yolks, honey, and Marsala in the top of a double boiler *over* (not touching) simmering water in the lower section of the double boiler until the sabayone becomes pale and foamy and has doubled in bulk. Serve the sauce at once over ice cream, fruit, or puddings.

Cream Sabayone Sauce. For a lighter and foamier sauce, fold ½ cup heavy cream, whipped, into the finished sauce.

VANILLA ICE CREAM SAUCE

1 pint vanilla ice cream   1 cup heavy cream, whipped

Place ice cream in refrigerator (not freezing compartment) for 1 hour or at room temperature for 15 minutes. Whip the cream in an electric beater, take it out, and whip the ice cream until it is smooth and soft. Fold in the whipped cream and serve the sauce at once with warm puddings.

CARAMEL SAUCE

1¼ cups light brown sugar   1¼ cups cream
¾ cup light corn syrup   2 teaspoons vanilla extract
2½ tablespoons unsalted
   butter

Boil sugar and syrup in a heavy pan until sugar is dissolved. Stir in the butter and cream and lower heat to simmer. Cook the sauce until it is as thick as heavy cream. Stir in the vanilla and serve hot over cold desserts. Keep the sauce warm or reheat it in the top of a double boiler over hot water.

FRUIT

We use fruit differently from other foods except in feeding it to our children and drinking fruit juice with our breakfasts. Otherwise we either forget about it or we push it into a few limited categories. We think of it first of all as a dessert, rarely as a first course, and more often for women and children than for men. It is associated with summer rather than winter, with luxury rather than economy. Finally we think of it as something vaguely laxative.

Fruit should play a leading part in healthful eating, and it should and can appear in every course—not at the same meal —but as part of different courses at different times. The first course is the healthiest place on the menu for fruit. Fruit makes beautiful salads alone or combined with vegetables, cheese, or any salad ingredients. First courses of melon, berries, oranges or grapefruit, or fruit cup can substitute for first-course salads. Watercress and apples is a classic combina-

182

tion, and so is endive and oranges. Fruit soups are popular in Scandinavia, and fruit with fish, meat, or poultry goes back to the figs and smoked ham of the ancient Romans. Fruit makes lovely sauces—meat never tastes better than with Cumberland sauce, and oranges are wedded to duck. Fruit breads are also excellent. There should be a fruit, a raw vegetable, and a cooked vegetable at every meal.

Store fresh fruit in a cool dry place or in the refrigerator after discarding unripe, bruised, or damaged fruit. Do not wash before storing.

See fruit recipes also among salads, soups, main courses, sauces, breads, desserts, and baking.

Fresh Fruit Desserts

Faring wisely is not just in eating. Wisdom also lies in selecting and preparing simple, effortless dishes so that the housewife need not eat her meals in a state of exhaustion. *Eating the healthiest foods when we are tense or tired is just as harmful as eating indigestible ones.* The uncomplicated preparations are recommended for their digestibility and because they spare the cook. A perfect way of achieving both these ends is to serve fruit and fruit desserts.

Fruits are healthful and most of them can be prepared ahead at leisure without last-minute processes. They are economical when the fruits are in season, and they taste extremely good besides.

Fruits and berries add vitamins, minerals, and bulk to our diet (more so when they are raw than when frozen or canned) and they are among the carbohydrates that are part of our daily requirement. Most of us eat fruit or drink fruit juice with breakfast and never give it another thought. Actually we should eat fruit and berries several times a day. When we eat them as dessert, they can be accompanied by honey, nuts, raisins, cheese, brown sugar. Eating wisely is not one bit less delicious than eating unwisely, and the fruit desserts that are listed are just as suitable for dinner parties as for home dinners.

The age-old dessert or "after table," a bowl of fruit, nuts, and dried fruits, is admirable. It can be accompanied, preceded, or followed by cheese. Every housewife should give her family an attractively served "after table" several times a week.

Fruits with sour cream and brown sugar were in vogue a few years ago. Many of us served seedless grapes or black cherries in this way, but when grapes and cherries were out of season we rarely looked farther. The combination is equally good with other fresh or preserved fruits and can be served all year round. Always whip the sour cream and add a little additional flavor with a squeeze of lemon juice or grated orange rind, or sieve the brown sugar with a little cinnamon.

PLUMS WITH SOUR CREAM

2 pounds small German plums, quartered lengthwise	2 cups sour cream, whipped ¼ cup brown sugar

1 pinch ground cinnamon

Prepare the fruit, chill it and serve it mixed with the sour cream, or pass cream and cinnamon-and-sugar mixture separately.

BLUEBERRIES AND GRAPES WITH SOUR CREAM

2 cups fresh blueberries	2 cups sour cream
1 cup stemmed green seedless grapes	3 drops vanilla extract
½ cup stemmed red currants, optional	¼ cup brown sugar
	1 pinch cinnamon

Combine the fruits and chill them in a crystal bowl. Whip the sour cream with the vanilla and pour it onto the center of the fruit. Pass a mixture of sugar and cinnamon separately.

BANANAS AND ORANGES WITH SOUR CREAM

3 large bananas, sliced across
1 orange and its grated rind
1 cup green seedless grapes

½ cup blueberries (omit in winter)
2 cups sour cream, whipped
¼ cup brown sugar

Grate orange rind onto a paper towel, peel the orange and separate into sections free from white membranes. Combine with grapes, blueberries, and bananas. Pour over the cream and sprinkle with brown sugar and grated orange rind.

The following fruits may be served with sour cream and brown sugar in the same way:

1. Green seedless grapes, add lemon juice or grated lemon rind to taste.
2. Sweet black cherries, add cinnamon to the brown sugar to taste.
3. Strawberries, add grated orange rind to taste.
4. Sliced peaches or apricots, add shaved blanched almonds to taste. Almonds may be toasted.
5. Sliced pears, add cinnamon to the brown sugar to taste.
6. Canned figs, add grated orange rind to the sour cream to taste.

Fresh fruit cups and salads, sweetened with honey if desired, may be served in any combination. Fruit salads are usually dressed with a sweet sauce or a French dressing. As neither is desirable because of sugar and condiments, use Fruit Salad Dressing, page 81, or Honey Dressing, page 84. With additions of cheese, a fruit salad makes a full and healthy meal. See Salads for more suggestions.

FRUITS IN LIME JUICE

4 peaches, peeled and
  sliced
3 pears, peeled and sliced
6 German plums, sliced
  lengthwise and pitted

1 to 2 cups seedless green
  grapes
4 limes
½ cup thin honey
1 sprig mint

Prepare fruit and arrange it in a bowl. Slice one lime for garnish and combine the juice of the remaining limes with the honey. Pour it over the fruit and serve very cold garnished with mint leaves.

MELON BALLS IN LIME JUICE

4 cups large melon balls:
  cantaloupe, water-
  melon, Persian, and
  honeydew

4 limes
½ cup finely chopped
  walnuts

Slice one lime for garnish, pour the juice of the remaining limes over the melon balls, and sprinkle with walnuts.

DRIED APPLES

Dried apples are suitable for applesauce, pies, cakes, and all recipes that call for stewed apples. An 8-ounce package will yield about 4 to 4⅓ cups cooked apples. Dried apple slices or rings are available in the dried-fruit section of most markets. They are treated with sulphur dioxide, which some consider to be harmful. Health-food stores sell *organic* dried apples at about twice the cost of sulphured dried apples. There are few *natural* dried apples available because they mold and deteriorate easily.

If dried at home, they must be heat and air dried. While a very low oven can do part of this, it is not properly ventilated for drying purposes, and the apples have to be taken out at intervals.

HOW TO DRY APPLES

Wash, peel, and core apples and slice them or cut them across into ⅛-inch rings. Make a solution of 1 tablespoon salt to 1 gallon water and soak the apple rings in it for 2 to 3 minutes. String the rings on a rod and let them drip, or spread apple slices on a towel. When they are dry, spread slices on a baking sheet or tray, leave rings on the rod, and dry them for periods in a very low oven and in the air.

The old method was to leave the apple slices or rings in a slowly cooling coal range overnight and in hot sun and air in the daytime. This method took 3 to 4 days to crisp the apples. Experiment with one or two apples before doing a larger quantity. Heat oven to lowest point on dial. Place the apples into it for a 4-hour period, then place them over a radiator in a warm room or over a radiator in a sunny window for 4 hours. Repeat until crisp. Left in an unventilated oven they will become limp but not crisp.

A dryer can be built for drying fruits and vegetables by making a ventilated cabinet with an electric heater placed under trays or rods of fruit. In this type of dryer, apples will be almost crisp in 8 to 10 hours. They are then stored in paper bags in air-tight containers and soaked in water or liquid before they are used. They should be inspected at intervals.

DESSERTS

HAZELNUT PUDDING

5 eggs, separated
⅓ cup light brown sugar
½ pound hazelnuts, finely
   ground
1 teaspoon vanilla

⅓ cup heavy cream
1 pinch cinnamon
¼ cup whole-wheat bread-
   crumbs

Beat egg yolks with the sugar until thick and creamy. Add the ground nuts gradually along with vanilla, cream, and cinnamon. Butter a pudding mold with a closely fitting lid and sprinkle the breadcrumbs into it. Close the mold and shake the breadcrumbs to adhere to the butter. Stir all superfluous crumbs into the pudding mixture. Whip the egg whites very stiff and fold them into the nut mixture. Fill the mold and cover tightly. It should fill ¾ of the mold. Steam the mold in a covered kettle of boiling water for 1 hour. Water in kettle should come ¾ way up the outside of the pudding mold. Unmold and serve with heavy cream.

CREME BRULEE

3 cups heavy cream,
   scalded
6 egg yolks

1 cup brown sugar
1 teaspoon vanilla

Beat the yolks with 6 tablespoons of the sugar until thick and creamy. Add the scalding cream in a thin stream, stirring constantly. Add vanilla and stir the custard in the top of a double boiler over simmering water until it coats the back of a spoon. Pour into a shallow heat-proof dish and chill until set. Sprinkle top with the remaining sugar. Depending on the size of the dish, more brown sugar may be needed to cover the surface thickly. Set the dish into a pan of ice cubes and push under the broiler. Revolve the dish with the help of pot holders so that the sugar can caramelize evenly. Watch it carefully as the sugar burns easily, especially if some part of it is a little higher than the rest. Chill the cream again and serve it cold.

FRENCH RICE PUDDING

½ cup brown rice
1 quart milk, scalded
3 tablespoons brown
   sugar

½ teaspoon vanilla
½ cup raisins
½ cup heavy cream

Combine all ingredients except the cream in the top of a double boiler over boiling water and cook for 1½ hours. Stir every 15 minutes and renew the water in the lower section of the double boiler as it boils away. Take rice from heat, beat in the cream and pour the pudding into a buttered baking dish. Bake at 350° F. until the top is brown, about 20 minutes. Chill and serve with a fruit sauce or heavy cream.

FROZEN CHEESE PIE

½ cup butter, melted
½ cup brown sugar
2 cups crushed graham
  crackers
1 teaspoon cinnamon
2 envelopes gelatin

Juice and grated rind of 1
  lemon
2 eggs, separated
1⅓ cups cream cheese at
  room temperature
½ cup heavy cream,
  whipped

Combine the butter, half the sugar, the cracker crumbs, and cinnamon and press ¾ of the mixture on the bottom and sides of an 8-inch pie pan. Chill until filling is ready. Stir gelatin with the lemon juice and set aside for 10 minutes. Stir egg yolks with the remaining brown sugar and ⅓ cup water in the top of a double boiler *over*—not touching—simmering water. Continue to stir until the mixture coats the back of a spoon. Take from heat and stir in the gelatin until it is dissolved. Beat egg yolk mixture and lemon rind slowly into cream cheese. Chill until mixture starts to set. Beat vigorously with a French wire whisk and fold in the stiffly beaten egg whites and the whipped cream. Pour into the pie crust and sprinkle with the remaining crumb mixture. Chill for at least 2 hours. Serve after it is set.

FRUIT INDIAN PUDDING

6 cups milk
½ cup stone-ground corn
  meal
1 cup molasses

½ cup chopped unsul-
  phured figs
½ cup raisins
1 beaten egg

2 tablespoons butter

Bring 2 cups of milk to a boil and pour into the top of a double boiler over boiling water. Stir in corn meal and cook, stirring occasionally, for 15 minutes. Add molasses, figs, and raisins and take from heat. Add 2 cups cold milk, beat in the egg and butter, and pour into a buttered baking dish. Bake at 250° F. for 30 minutes, then add the last 2 cups cold milk and continue to bake for another 2½ hours. Serve at once with whipped cream.

PEACH TRIFLE

6 slices stale sponge cake
Juice and grated rind of 2
  oranges
4 cups sliced stewed peaches

4 egg whites
½ cup walnuts, finely
  chopped
¼ cup light brown sugar

Line a heat-proof serving dish or deep pie pan with slices of sponge cake sprinkled with orange juice. Cover the cake with peach slices and sprinkle over orange rind and half the brown sugar. Whip egg whites stiff, fold in walnuts and remaining sugar, and spread the meringue over the peaches. Brown quickly under a broiler and serve.

PEACH PUDDING

6 ripe peaches, scalded,
  peeled, halved, and
  pitted
4 eggs, separated
⅔ cup light brown sugar

1 teaspoon baking powder
1 teaspoon vanilla
1½ cups graham cracker
  crumbs

Arrange peach halves cut side down in a buttered baking dish. Beat yolks with sugar and baking powder until creamy, add vanilla and graham cracker crumbs, and fold in stiffly beaten egg whites. Pour mixture over peaches and bake at 350° F. for about 40 minutes, or until puffed and brown.

PLUM WHOLE-WHEAT BETTY
(can be made with peaches, apricots, or apples)

3 cups stale whole-wheat breadcrumbs
⅓ cup butter
½ to ⅔ cups brown sugar, to taste

1 pinch cinnamon to taste
4 cups blue plums, pitted and sliced
5 tablespoons orange juice or any fruit juice

Crush or roughly grind enough stale whole-wheat bread to make 2½ cups of crumbs. Fry in the butter over medium heat until lightly browned. Stir cinnamon and sugar together. Spread a layer of crumbs in the bottom of a buttered 1½-quart baking dish and cover with a layer of plums. Sprinkle with the sugar and continue in this way using up all the ingredients and ending with a layer of crumbs. Sprinkle with fruit juice and bake at 350° F. for about 30 minutes or until browned. Serve with heavy cream.

BROWN-SUGAR BETTY

1 cup raisins
2 tablespoons apple cider, plus enough to cover the raisins
5 apples, peeled and cored
1 teaspoon cinnamon
¼ cup butter

½ teaspoon powdered cloves
2 lemons, grated rind and juice
2 cups graham cracker crumbs
1 cup dark brown sugar

Soak the raisins in cider overnight. Mix the spices and lemon rind. Cut apples across into thin slices. Butter a baking dish and put in a layer of graham cracker crumbs, then a layer of apple slices. Sprinkle with the spices and lemon rind and spread a few raisins over it. Sprinkle sugar over the raisins and put in another layer of cracker crumbs. Continue until all the ingredients are used up ending with a layer of cracker crumbs. Pour over the butter, melted with the 2 tablespoons of cider and the juice of the lemons. Bake at 350° F. for about 40 minutes, until browned. Serve warm with heavy cream or Devonshire Cream.

BAKED BANANAS

Peel and cut 9 bananas in half lengthwise and arrange them in a buttered baking dish. Sprinkle with ½ cup brown sugar and ½ cup orange juice and bake at 350° F. until tender and browned, about 12 minutes.

BANANA MERINGUES

6 large unpeeled bananas ¼ cup finely chopped pecans
4 egg whites ¼ cup light brown sugar
Butter for pan

Cut bananas in half lengthwise, scoop the meat out of the skins carefully, mash it, and return it to the shells. Beat the egg whites stiff. Fold in nuts and spread or pipe the meringue onto the length of the bananas. Arrange in a shallow buttered pan, sprinkle with the brown sugar, and put into a hot 400° F. oven for about 10 minutes or until they are browned.

BAKED PEARS

6 large, hard pears, ¼ cup chopped almonds
 peeled ¼ cup chopped raisins
1¼ cups light brown sugar 1 pinch each powered cloves
⅓ cup toasted wheat   and cinnamon
 germ 3 tablespoons honey

Boil 1 cup of sugar with 1½ cups water for 5 minutes. Combine wheat germ, almonds, raisins, spices, and the remaining ¼ cup of the sugar. Bind mixture with honey. Cut a piece off the bottom of each pear so it will stand upright. Cut pears across at the point where they widen. Scoop out the cores with a melon ball cutter and fill with wheat germ mixture. Return tops of the pears and secure with wooden picks. Stand pears in a baking dish and pour over the syrup. Bake at 325° F., basting frequently with the syrup, for about 1 hour. Cool pears slightly in the dish, remove picks, and serve warm with heavy cream.

APPLE NUT PIE

8 tart green apples,
  peeled and cored
1½ cups brown sugar
1 teaspoon cinnamon

½ cup chopped pecans
½ cup butter
1 cup very finely ground
  almonds

1 cup heavy cream

Slice the apples thin and layer them in a 9-inch pie pan. Sprinkle with 1 cup of the brown sugar mixed with cinnamon and pecans. Cream the butter, stir in the remaining brown sugar, and work in the ground almonds. Drop this mixture over the pecans and spread it with a moistened spatula or moistened hands. Bake the pie at 350° F. for 45 minutes or until lightly browned. Cool and serve with heavy cream or whipped cream.

APPLES IN PAPER

6 large baking apples
1 cup brown sugar
½ cup raisins, chopped
Juice and grated rind of 1
  lemon

1 cup ground hazelnuts
½ cup butter, creamed
1 cup heavy cream,
  whipped

Pare apples and scoop out the cores. Fill with ½ cup brown sugar mixed with raisins, lemon juice, and rind. Place filled apples into 6 heat-proof baking dishes and have ready 6 brown or parchment paper bags. Mix remaining sugar and nuts and stir into the butter. Divide mixture into 6 parts and put one on the top of each apple. Push each dish into a paper bag. Close securely and bake on a baking sheet at 400° F. until paper is brown and brittle and apples are tender, about 50 minutes. Serve the apples in the packages on dessert plates. The paper should be cut away at the table. Pass whipped cream or heavy cream separately.

Frozen desserts that contain cream and eggs can be sweetened with brown sugar, honey, or raw sugar. They are healthful in moderation, except when weight is being controlled. They are far more healthful, especially for children, than commercial ice creams.

MAPLE MOUSSE

4 eggs, separated	2 cups heavy cream,
1 cup pure maple syrup	whipped
½ cup chopped walnuts	

Stir the yolks and syrup in the top of a double boiler over simmering water until thickened. Remove from heat and beat mixture until cold. Chill. Beat the egg whites stiff, and fold into syrup mixture with the whipped cream. Dip mold into cold water, pour in the mousse, and freeze in the deep freezer or in the freezing compartment of the refrigerator. To unmold, dip for a moment in hot water and invert the mousse onto a cold platter. Let stand in the refrigerator for a few minutes to soften very slightly and sprinkle with nuts before serving.

BISCUIT TORTONI

2 eggs, separated
½ cup raw sugar
1 teaspoon vanilla extract
1 teaspoon almond
  extract

2 cups heavy cream
½ cup finely ground toasted
  cashew nuts or
  almonds

Beat the yolks with half the sugar until very thick and light and then beat in the flavorings. Beat the egg whites until half stiff, then gradually beat in remaining sugar until stiff. Whip the cream very stiff. Fold egg whites into the yolks and then fold in whipped cream. Put into paper cases, ramekins, or a soufflé dish and freeze 30 minutes in deep freeze or freezing compartment of refrigerator. Sprinkle with nuts and freeze at least 2 hours longer.

BAKING BREAD

The basic ingredients of bread, flour, water, and yeast have remained very much the same since the ancient Egyptians discovered fermentation and the Romans obtained their leaven from wine mold and pressed it into little cakes. The water has been changed to various combinations of liquids, and the yeast cakes, or dry yeast, have been standardized, but the controversies over flour have come and gone through the centuries, mostly about its color and what that color stood for. White bread was for rich men, brown bread was peasant fare. Dark breads were popular in central Europe, but most Englishmen and Americans wanted white bread, the whiter the better. Their wishes have been fulfilled with snow-white loaves, light, sliced, and long-lived. But the nourishment, with the exception of the endosperm, has been taken out and, by government order, it has been replaced by enrichments. The fault for our loaves today does not lie with the mills or the government, it lies with *us*—we demanded and they complied. Now

197

we are bread-conscious again and, while we can buy excellent whole-wheat and bran breads, sprouted-wheat, rye and dark breads, we are also baking again.

It should be noted that the large bakeries and the small bakers are filling the demand for whole-grain breads with excellent products. Sprouted-wheat breads, rye and whole-wheat breads are available in all markets and bakeries. They contain, as shown on the wrappers, stone-ground whole-wheat flour, sprouted-wheat kernels, raw wheat germ, honey, soybean oil, brown sugar, fresh yeast, unsulphured molasses, dried sunflower seeds, sesame seeds, and lemon juice. The ingredients are above reproach and the flavor and texture are excellent.

While home-baked bread is incomparable, it must be borne in mind that the whole-grain flours vary, depending on whether they are stone-ground, the area where they are grown, and storage before use. They deteriorate easily and should never be bought in large quantities. Baking whole-grain breads successfully at home means care, a greater amount of kneading, and accurate times and temperatures for rising. Recipes can never be absolutely precise and the housewife may have to experiment before she can bake the perfect health loaf. A few years ago it was hard to find dark breads on market shelves, but now they are not only available, but of good taste and quality.

At one time the housewife ground grain, like coffee beans, in a home mill just before she used it. Now we can buy or mail-order stone-ground whole-grain flours for home baking. When white flour is milled all the most healthful parts, and the brownest, are removed—wheat germ and bran. The vitamin B that is removed with the wheat germ is partly returned with the enrichments. We can take additional vitamin B pills, but it is much better to eat a slice of good full-kernel bread each day than to swallow a pill. The only reason that our white bread is not responsible for greater ill health is that we eat a more varied diet than before. Our living standard is higher and we no longer live on bread alone—but we should not try to live without it.

WHOLE-WHEAT BREAD

2 cups milk, scalded	2 cups lukewarm water,
⅓ cup honey	about 80° F.
1 tablespoon sea salt	10 cups whole-wheat flour
3 cakes compressed yeast	⅓ cup oil

Put scalded milk in a large bowl, add honey and salt, and let cool to lukewarm. Dissolve yeast in lukewarm water and add to the lukewarm milk. Stir in 5 cups of flour, add oil, and stir in remaining flour. Cover and set in a warm (80 to 85° F.), draft-free place. Let rise until doubled in bulk, about 1 hour. Knead the dough very lightly on a board, using as little whole-wheat flour on the board as possible. Leave dough on the board and cover with a cloth. Let rise a second time until almost doubled in bulk, about 40 minutes. Shape into 3 loaves and place into 3 large, buttered bread pans. Cover and let stand 30 minutes longer. Bake at 375° F. for about 1 hour.

GLUTEN BREAD

1 cup milk, scalded	1 cup lukewarm water,
1 tablespoon raw sugar	about 80° F.
1 tablespoon sea salt	4 cups gluten flour
1 cake compressed yeast	1 tablespoon oil

Put scalded milk in a large bowl, add sugar and salt, and cool to lukewarm. Dissolve yeast in lukewarm water and add it to lukewarm milk. Beat in 2 cups of flour until smooth, add oil and remaining flour. Knead dough lightly and quickly until smooth and elastic. Rinse and dry the bowl, oil lightly and return dough to it. Cover with a cloth and set in a warm (80 to 85° F.), draft-free place until doubled in bulk, about 1¾ hours. Divide dough in half, shape into loaves and place into 2 buttered bread pans. Cover and let rise again until double in bulk, about 1 hour. Bake at 400° F. for about 45 minutes.

SWEDISH RYE BREAD
(Limpe)

½ cup brown sugar
2 teaspoons caraway seeds
1 teaspoon ground anise
   seed
1 tablespoon grated
   orange rind

1 tablespoon oil
2 cups boiling water
1 cake compressed yeast
2½ cups whole-wheat flour
2 teaspoons sea salt
2½ cups rye flour

Add sugar, caraway seeds, anise, orange rind, and oil to boiling water and boil until sugar is dissolved, about 3 minutes. Take from heat, pour into a large bowl, and cool to lukewarm, about 80° F. Crumble yeast over the mixture and stir well until dissolved. Stir in whole-wheat flour, little by little, to make a soft dough. Cover with a cloth and place in a warm (80 to 85° F.), draft-free place, and let rise for 1½ hours. Work in salt and rye flour to make a stiff dough. Let rise again for 2 hours. Knead lightly and shape into a loaf. Place in an oiled 9 x 5 x 3 inch bread pan and let rise again for 35 minutes. Bake at 350° F. for about 1 hour.

FINNISH RYE BREAD

1 tablespoon brown
   sugar
2 teaspoons sea salt
2 tablespoons margarine
1½ cups boiling water
1 cake compressed
   yeast

½ cup warm water, 105 to
   115° F.
3 cups rye flour
2 to 3 cups whole-wheat
   flour
½ teaspoon ground caraway
   seeds, optional

Place sugar, salt, and margarine in a large bowl. Take boiling water from heat and as soon as it stops boiling, pour into the bowl and let cool to lukewarm. Measure the ½ cup of warm water into a small bowl and crumble yeast over it. Stir until dissolved. Pour yeast into the lukewarm mixture and beat in rye flour until smooth. Stir in 2 cups of whole-wheat flour and the caraway seeds and add just enough additional flour to make a soft dough. Turn out onto a lightly floured board and knead until elastic, about 10 minutes. Put back into an oiled bowl, turning it to oil all sides of the dough. Cover with a towel and let rise in a warm (80 to 85° F.), draft-free place until doubled in bulk, about 45 minutes. Punch down the dough, divide in half, and shape into 2 loaves. Put into 2 oiled 9 x 5 x 3 inch bread pans and cover with a cloth. Return to the warm place and let rise again until doubled in bulk, about 40 minutes. Bake at 400° F. for about 30 minutes. Let one loaf cool, but serve one of them warm. Cut slices as thin as possible, spread with butter at room temperature and clear or granulated honey. The bread may also be sliced on the next day and parched in a 200° F. oven.

WHOLE-WHEAT MUFFINS

1 ½ cups whole-wheat flour	1 teaspoon sea salt
3 tablespoons brown sugar	1 tablespoon baking powder
	1 large egg, beaten
	⅔ cup milk

3 tablespoons melted butter

Measure flour, sugar, salt, and baking powder into a medium bowl. Stir well. Beat egg, milk, and butter together and stir into dry ingredients until they are just bound but not smooth. Fill a well-buttered or oiled miniature muffin tin and bake at 375° F. for about 20 minutes or until muffins are done and loose in the pan. Yield: 12 miniature muffins. Serve hot with cold butter.

WHOLE-WHEAT POPOVERS

2½ tablespoons oil   ¼ cup melted butter
4 eggs   2 cups milk
Sea salt, to taste,   1¼ cups stone-ground
    optional   whole-wheat flour

Spoon about 1 teaspoon oil into 8 large custard cups or iron popover forms. If custard cups are used, place them on a baking sheet and heat at 475° F. for about 1½ minutes. Blend or beat eggs, salt, and melted butter until smooth. Stir in flour and divide batter, filling cups about ¾ full. Bake at 475° F. for about 20 minutes. Reduce heat to 350° F. and bake 20 to 25 minutes longer. Serve at once, or pierce with a fork and let dry in the turned-off oven for a few minutes longer.

To transpose existing bread-baking recipes to the healthful ingredients we are now using, follow these rules:

1. Substitute approximately ¾ cup whole-grain flour for 1 cup of white all-purpose flour.

2. Depending on the type and texture of the whole-grain flour, the liquids may have to be increased about 1 tablespoon to a cup. Whole-grain breads require about 2 cups liquid to every 6 cups flour.

3. The liquids for whole-grain breads can be milk, potato water, stock, soy milk, fruit juices, or tomato juice.

4. Reduce the amount of oil used in white breads by about ⅓ when baking whole-grain breads. Use sunflower, safflower, soy, linseed, or other oils in preference to peanut oil in baking bread. Oil may be substituted for butter on a tablespoon-for-tablespoon basis.

5. When using honey or molasses instead of refined sugar, honey may be slightly reduced or used measure for measure. Molasses should be reduced by about ⅓.

6. The whole-grain breads are enhanced by flavors. Caraway seeds, grated orange or lemon rind, ground anise or fennel seeds, cardamon, raisins, dates, or nuts may be added.

7. Experiment with various combinations of flours, ground soybeans, and sunflower seed meal. Substitute a small quantity of wheat germ or nutritional yeast for some of the flour.

8. Knead whole-grain breads longer, use as little flour on the bread board as possible, and do not let the bread rise for quite as long a period as white bread recipes require.

9. Buy whole-grain flours in smaller quantities than all-purpose flour, and buy stone-ground whole-grain flours whenever possible.

10. Shape and cool the loaves as any white bread, but do not store them for as long a period.

11. In using yeast for healthful bread baking, try to use compressed yeast in preference to dry yeast, if compressed yeast is available.

12. For quick breads, some people prefer the old and famous Rumford baking powder that is again obtainable in health-food stores and markets.

IMPORTED BREADS

If your market or organic-food store carries the imported packaged breads *Vollkorn Brot* or *Waerland Brot* be sure to eat at least one slice a day. *Waerland Brot* follows the recipe of Scandinavian food-reform pioneer Are Waerland and is baked of naturally grown whole grains according to strict specifications. *Friesen Brot* comes from Northern Germany and is also a *Vollkorn* (whole-grain) bread. Linseed bread and graham flour bread are well-distributed imports.

Swedish Limpe, Scandinavian flat breads, and whole-grain wafers are also well distributed and obtainable in Scandinavian bakeries. Another excellent bread, Lebanese bread, can be found in many areas. This is especially good when split and toasted.

All the imported breads are foil and cellophane wrapped, sliced in small packages, or packed in the whole loaf. Some of the whole-grain breads are canned, as are some of the pumpernickels. The central Europeans and Scandinavians have always eaten the dark whole-grain breads, although city dwellers have followed the trend toward the light loaves.

If the bread should go stale, it can be grated or blended into crumbs for desserts, to sprinkle over applesauce, or to use in stuffings.

APPETIZERS, CANAPES, AND SANDWICHES

Salty appetizers and thirst-arousing foods are not really part of a healthful eating program. Nor are rich hors d'oeuvres and canapés at the beginning of a meal. The salted nuts, potato chips, anchovies, and green olives that taste so good before dinner often account for more than a day's allowance of salt. They are designed to stimulate the appetite for more food and drink, but they often supply us with as many calories as the dinner that follows. Some foods, however, should be eaten as appetizers—but *instead of* rather than *before* the first dinner course.

Healthful eating need not conflict with entertaining; it is better to serve these healthy foods than to watch the scales after every dinner party. Raw vegetables—the crudities— should be eaten before dinner, and salads and fruits should always come before the main course. There is no reason why these health measures should not become part of the appetizer tray rather than the highly spiced concoctions we usually serve.

Sandwiches, on the other hand, are an important part of healthful eating, in the school lunch box, for home luncheons, for tea, for light suppers, and picnics. Small sandwiches are perfect for some parties and a large sandwich can be a meal in itself. The important thing is that the bread should never dominate the filling. If the bread is right, and if the double and triple-deckers are limited to the children, hearty sandwiches to the men, and open-faced sandwiches to the women, then they have a place in healthful eating.

Appetizers

Serve all the raw vegetables by themselves or in combination with seafood or meat. Fruits can be served raw or in combinations. The following recipes do not include smoked meats or fish or highly spiced or salted foods, but they do include eggs and cheese. Always remember that they count as part of your daily food requirement, and calories eaten before dinner must be subtracted from dinner. The raw vegetables are low in calories but salted nuts and smoked fish are high. Always try to serve celery stalks, carrot sticks, cherry tomatoes in season, radishes, raw cucumber, zucchini, or cauliflower. Other raw vegetables can be marinated before they are served.

FRENCH MUSHROOMS

1 pound medium mushrooms	2 tablespoons finely chopped parsley
¾ cup French Dressing	½ clove garlic, crushed
2 tablespoons finely chopped onion	1 tablespoon lemon juice

Clean mushrooms with a soft, damp cloth, trim the stems level with the caps, and slice the mushrooms thin. Save stems to use in soup. Combine the remaining ingredients, pour them over the mushrooms, and let them marinate in the refrigerator for at least 2 hours. Turn them gently every half hour. When they are wilted and dark, strain off the marinade and serve the mushrooms with lightly buttered whole-grain bread.

STUFFED MUSHROOMS

24 medium small mush-
    rooms
½ cup crumbled Roque-
    fort cheese

2 tablespoons sour cream
2 teaspoons minced onion
3 tablespoons minced parsley

Clean raw mushrooms with a damp cloth. If discolored, peel them carefully. Trim ends off stems and break stems out of the caps. Chop stems and beat with cheese, sour cream, and onion. Fill caps with mixture and sprinkle with parsley.

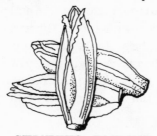

STUFFED ENDIVE

3 to 4 stalks Belgian
    endive
¾ cup crushed Roquefort
    cheese at room tem-
    perature

2 tablespoons sour cream
1 tablespoon mayonnaise
½ teaspoon scraped onion

Trim the endive and separate into leaves. Crush the cheese with the other ingredients and beat until smooth. Add sour cream if necessary to make a spreadable paste. Put about a tablespoon into each endive leaf and serve.

The same cheese paste may be used to stuff trimmed celery stalks.

CUCUMBER OR ZUCCHINI SLICES

2 straight, evenly sized
　cucumbers or zucchini
3 ounces cream cheese, at
　room temperature

2 tablespoons sour cream
½ tablespoon minced onion
2 tablespoons finely cut
　chives

Score cucumber with a fluted knife and cut it across into even, thin slices, about 1/5 inch thick. Cut zucchini in the same way but do not score. Dry slices on paper kitchen towels and top each with a small pyramid of cheese stirred with sour cream and onion. Sprinkle cheese with chives and serve.

WALNUT CHEESE BALL

8 ounces sharp Cheddar
　cheese

6 ounces cream cheese
6 ounces Bleu cheese

2 cups chopped walnuts

Bring all cheeses to room temperature and put them through a meat grinder or mash with a fork. Stir to mix well and shape into a ball. Roll in the walnuts until they completely cover the surface of the cheese. Wrap in wax paper and chill for at least 2 hours. Serve with a knife and rye bread rounds or rye crackers. The ball can be garnished with parsley or crisp watercress.

GUACAMOLE

3 avocados
2 limes
1 lemon
1 small onion, minced
2 tablespoons mayonnaise

½ teaspoon celery seeds
¼ cup chopped pecans
Freshly ground black
　pepper

As close to serving as possible, juice 1 of the limes and grate the rind from the lemon. Juice the lemon and add to the lime juice. Combine with onion, mayonnaise, celery seed, and pecans. At the last moment cut the avocados in half, remove pits, and crush the meat with the first mixture. Season with pepper to taste and return the mixture to one or two of the avocado shells. Garnish with the second lime, thinly sliced, and serve with corn crisps or thin wheat crackers.

CARROTS AND ONION CHEESE

3 or 4 long straight carrots	½ onion, minced
6 ounces cream cheese, at room temperature	¼ cup mayonnaise
	1 tablespoon cut chives

Scrape carrots and cut into wide, thin sticks. Chill in water until needed. Whip cream cheese with onion and mayonnaise, adding more mayonnaise if necessary to make a soft, smooth dip. Put into a shallow bowl, sprinkle the center with chives, and push the carrot sticks into the cheese so that they can be used as a vehicle for the cheese.

PARCHED NUTS

Used shelled filberts, hazelnuts, walnuts, pecans, or scalded almonds for this purpose. Place the nuts in a single layer on a baking sheet and parch or dry them in a 200° F. oven until crisp and golden. Shake them at intervals to brown evenly. The size and age of the nuts influence the length of time it will take to parch them. When done they should be brittle and dry and will become cream colored and golden. When they are pale golden they must be watched as they turn brown and bitter very quickly. Walnuts and pecans take less time than almonds and filberts. Large nuts can take an entire morning to become really dry. If the heat is increased they will brown before they are thoroughly dried out. Drying takes patience but the result is worthwhile.

Parching will loosen the brown inner skins of filberts or hazelnuts. Much of it can be rubbed off with a rough kitchen towel after the nuts have been in the oven for about 1 hour or as soon as the skins start to drop from some of the nuts.

Canapés

Canapé is the French word for a couch, and a canapé is literally a small couch of bread with something resting on it, rather like a miniature open sandwich.

Trim crusts from 8 pieces of thin-sliced whole-wheat bread and butter them lightly. Cut into triangles, oblongs, rounds, fingers, or rectangles. Spread a base onto the canapés and garnish according to any of the suggestions below.

For the base, use either cream cheese or butter. Cream cheese may be stirred with chopped walnuts, watercress, pimento, cucumber, mushrooms, or ripe olives. Butter should be stirred with grated lemon rind or orange rind, mild brown mustard, minced parsley, chives, or shrimp. If cheese or butter are too soft after stirring, chill them until they reach a good spreading consistency.

Garnish the bases as follows:

Walnut cheese base with minced watercress
Watercress cheese with crumbled crisp bacon
Pimento cheese with ½ black pitted olive
Cucumber cheese with ½ walnut
Mushroom cheese with a strip of radish slices
Olive cheese with slices of stuffed olives

Lemon butter with half a shrimp, cut lengthwise
Orange butter with a cooked asparagus tip
Mustard butter with a sliver of rare roast beef
Parsley butter with a wedge of raw apple
Chive butter with a small raw cauliflower rosette
Shrimp butter with a cucumber slice and dill

Sandwiches

Use whole-wheat and other whole-grain or rye breads, sprouted-wheat bread, or pumpernickel. Trim off the crusts for small sandwiches, but leave them on for children's and men's sandwiches. Crusts help to keep sandwiches from drying out. The bread may be plain or toasted and can be spread lightly with butter, margarine, or mayonnaise.

Sandwich fillings are divided into several categories. There are the straightforward, healthful sliced meat and/or cheese sandwiches:

Chicken	Roast beef	Ham
Turkey	Roast pork	Baked ham
Swiss cheese	Roast lamb	Tongue

These sandwiches are improved and less dry when they are made with lettuce leaves or thinly sliced cucumbers or tomatoes.

Salad sandwiches are often made of leftovers that are diced or chopped and bound with mayonnaise before they are thickly spread on the bread. They are also improved with a lettuce leaf, and the mayonnaise may be lightly flavored to enhance the mixture:

Egg salad	Shrimp salad
Sliced eggs	Salmon salad
Chicken salad	Other fish salads

Vegetable sandwiches such as tomato, cucumber, or lettuce are especially good when a variety of sandwiches are being served. Chopped watercress is excellent.

Sandwiches filled with spreads, such as mixtures of cream cheese or liver paste, also tend to be a little dry if they are not made with lettuce leaves.

Freshly cooked sandwich ingredients such as bacon, chicken livers, eggs, or melted cheese have to be eaten on the spot. They are among the healthful sandwiches, but meats that have been reheated in thick gravy and poured over slices of bread are not.

Hamburger sandwiches, which are customarily served on a toasted bun, are as good as they are popular. Children want the whole bun, some adults leave off half the bun, but the 60 percent of Americans over forty who have become weight-conscious are better off with the hamburger without any of the bun.

Tea sandwiches are traditionally thin with crusts trimmed off. The bread may be sliced very thin or it can be slightly weighted or lightly rolled with a rolling pin. Fillings are usually lettuce, cucumbers, watercress, thinly sliced meats, and delicate pastes.

Open-faced sandwiches have the advantage, for adults, of having half as much bread. They are *arranged* rather than spread or filled, and some of them are piled high with scrambled eggs, shrimp, and garnishes. A fork and knife is needed to eat many of them.

The Scandinavian open-faced sandwich, which is a cross between a sandwich, a still-life, and a canapé, particularly lends itself to the new healthful dark breads. The dark breads have distinct textures and flavors of their own, which change and enhance the topping or filling of the sandwich. As a result, many people are taking a new interest in sandwiches and serving them more often.

No healthful eating program favors the eating of too much bread, but the dark full-kernel breads are *required eating,* and two open-faced sandwiches are the equivalent of one double decker. Full-kernel breads have a nutlike flavor, are sliced much thinner than white sandwich breads, and the slices are smaller.

The open sandwich is decorative and explanatory. We can bite into it without pressing down a top slice and squeezing the content out of the opposite side. The men who prepare the sandwiches at the luncheon counters put unscrupulous amounts of lettuce, tomatoes, bacon—anything—on a slice of bread. They hide it all under the top slice, press it down lightly, cut it across, and often pin it down with wooden picks. The bursts of mayonnaise and bits of hard-cooked egg are up to the luncher to take care of. The open-faced sandwich never collapses into disarray. It is neat, overt, and you eat half as much. It is the age-old lunch of the Scandinavians, the food their children grow on and businessmen take to work.

Everyone has a talent for composing them with unexpected ingredients. I recently was given a slice of Waerland Bread with a breath of butter, a thin slice of cooked celery root, a slice of hard-cooked egg, and a little glob of vegetable salad bound with mayonnaise. The author of the sandwich was a doctor, and I have no doubt it was a well-thought-out and balanced luncheon, since there was a sprinkling of chopped walnuts. Needless to say it was delicious, and while I thought it rather skimpy, it sustained me for the whole afternoon.

AN OPEN-SANDWICH LUNCHEON

4 slices Are Waerland full-kernel bread
3 tablespoons butter
1 thin slice cold roast beef
1 thin slice munster cheese
3 cooked shrimp cut through lengthwise
1 hard-cooked egg, sliced
2 tablespoons cream cheese whipped with a little sour cream
2 teaspoons cut chives
1 small dill pickle cut into a fan of slices

½ small tomato, sliced
1 sardine or 2 sprats, drained
1 red radish, sliced
Sprigs of dill, parsley, and watercress
1 tablespoon pickled beets cut in matchsticks
3 paper-thin onion slices
4 small red radish roses
Lettuce leaves
4 cucumber slices

Spread the bread slices with butter and cover one with beef, one with cheese, another with the shrimps fanned out three halves to a side, and the last with overlapping egg slices. Pipe soft cream cheese in the center of the shrimp sandwich and cover with cut chives. Lay the pickle slices on the beef, sliced tomatoes on the cheese, and the sardine across the sliced eggs. Decorate the sandwiches with radish slices and sprigs of dill, parsley, or watercress. Finish the beef sandwich with little matchsticks of pickled beets, and the cheese sandwich with onion slices between the overlapping tomato slices. Garnish the open sandwich plate with lettuce leaves, cucumber slices, and small radish roses.

BEVERAGES

The perfect, unequaled health beverage is fresh spring water. Some people are thirstier than others, namely those who eat a great many candies and sweets, but the same rule applies to water as to food. *Drink when you are thirsty.* Drink water between meals, *not during meals,* and drink at least 1 quart a day. Some doctors still urge 2 quarts of water a day, but others feel that the system can become waterlogged. Much depends on climate, exercise, and diet, but the most important thing is to drink water when you feel thirsty.

The *healthy drinks* are the beverages, dairy drinks, teas, and fruit juices that are beneficial to health. Among them are tomato juice and vegetable juices. *Health drinks* are also sold that have specific beneficial properties.

Serve all fruit juices and healthy drinks immediately after preparing them. They lose in value when they stand.

VEGETABLE JUICE I

3 cups cold tomato juice
3 sprigs parsley
2 stalks celery, cut into
   short pieces
½ cucumber, sliced
½ green pepper, seeded
   and sliced

½ onion, sliced
Juice and outside yellow rind
   of ½ lemon
1 slice whole-wheat bread,
   broken into pieces
1 lemon, quartered

Blend all ingredients and add tomato juice if it is too thick. Serve garnished with lemon quarters.

VEGETABLE JUICE II

3 cups cold tomato juice
2 stalks celery, cut into
   short lengths

3 lettuce leaves
6 spinach leaves
1 curl lemon peel

Blend all ingredients and add tomato juice if it is too thick.

FRESH TOMATO JUICE

12 ripe tomatoes, about 3
   pounds
1½ cups chopped celery
¼ cup chopped green
   pepper

2 tablespoons chopped onion
4 parsley sprigs, chopped
½ bay leaf
1 teaspoon sea salt, optional

Quarter tomatoes and cut out stem ends. Place all ingredients in a heavy kettle over low heat and simmer, shaking frequently until the juices have gathered. Cook until tomatoes and celery are very soft, from 20 to 40 minutes depending on ripeness of the tomatoes. Press through a sieve or food mill, or blend until smooth. Chill and shake before serving. The juice may be strained once more after blending. Serve with lemon wedges.

Some health drinks, besides those already mentioned, are:

Bottled Spring Waters	**Bottled Fresh Fruit Juices**
Mountain Valley	Apple juice
Poland	Fresh apple cider
Perrier	Plum juice
Vichy	Grape juice

Fruit Juices

Fruit juices are unequaled in their benefits and should be a part of the menu at least twice a day. Drink them fresh, unsweetened, and undiluted.

The only thing better are the whole fruits. Eat fruit at breakfast, as a first course at meals, between meals, and when dieting. Drink fruit juices as refreshers in summer and thirst-quenchers in summer, but do not drink them in preference to eating fresh fruit.

PRUNE JUICE

3 cups iced prune juice   1 tablespoon lemon juice, or
2 eggs   to taste
4 lemon slices

Shake or blend until smooth, pour into 4 juice glasses, and garnish with the lemon slices.

ORANGE JUICE

3 cups cold orange juice   3 egg yolks
1 tablespoon honey

Blend all ingredients and serve in juice glasses.

MIXED FRUIT JUICES

Juice of 2 oranges
Juice of 1 grapefruit
1 cup apple juice

1 ripe pear, peeled, cored,
and cut in pieces
Fresh mint

Blend and serve in juice glasses garnished with mint sprigs.

LEMONADE

12 lemons
Grated rind of 3 of the
lemons

Sugar syrup to taste,
page 219
8 mint sprigs for garnish

Grate rind off 3 of the lemons and slice 1 lemon for garnish. Squeeze the 3 grated and the remaining 8 lemons to produce 1¾ to 2 cups lemon juice. Remove pits but do not strain the juice. Combine with sugar syrup to taste and chill until needed. Pour about ½ cup cold lemon syrup over ice cubes or crushed ice in 8 tall glasses. Fill with cold water or soda water, stir, and garnish with lemon slices and mint.

LIMEADE

1 cup fresh lime juice
4 cups cold fresh water or 1
quart sparkling water

½ cup sugar syrup

If sugar syrup is not available, heat ¼ cup brown sugar with ½ cup cold water and stir until sugar is dissolved. Boil unstirred for 5 minutes, cool and add to lime juice. Chill. Pour over ice in 6 tall glasses and fill with water.

ORANGEADE

1 cup fresh orange juice
Juice of 1 lime
3 cups fresh cold water

¼ to ½ cup sugar syrup to
taste
1 orange, sliced

Follow recipe for limeade and garnish the glasses with orange slices.

APPLE-MINT ADE

1 small bunch mint	2 cups apple juice, chilled
1 cup raw sugar	1 cup lime juice, chilled
1 cup fresh water	1 pint sparkling water

Select the tops of the 6 best mint sprigs for garnish. Remove the stems and chop the remaining mint leaves fine. Stir sugar and water together in a heavy pan over low heat until sugar is dissolved. Increase heat and boil without stirring for 8 minutes. Pour the sugar syrup over the mint leaves and let them steep as the syrup cools. Add apple juice and lime juice and pour into tall glasses filled with ice cubes. Garnish each glass with a mint sprig and fill with sparkling water.

SPICED APPLE JUICE

If you live near a cider mill, get fresh apple juice in autumn and serve it hot.

2 gallons apple juice	3 cinnamon sticks
1⅔ cups brown sugar	1 tablespoon cloves
½ tablespoon allspice	

Heat apple juice, add the sugar, and stir until it dissolves. Add spices and simmer for 20 minutes. Serve hot in mugs with handles.

Fruit ades and combination drinks all require some sweetening to be palatable, whereas fruit juices should not be sweetened unless absolutely necessary. The sweetening agents can be brown sugar, raw sugar, or honey, but the easiest way to use sugars is in the form of a syrup. Sugars are not affected by boiling, but heat destroys some of the enzymes in honey. Whenever possible shake or blend beverages that are sweetend with honey until it is dissolved.

SUGAR SYRUP

2 cups brown or raw sugar   1 cup cold water

Pour sugar into a heavy pan. Add fresh cold water and stir over low heat until sugar is dissolved. Increase the heat and boil without stirring for about 10 minutes or until a candy thermometer registers 220° F. Cool and store in a tightly covered jar in a cool cupboard.

Tea

The world has produced three major nonalcoholic beverages—the extracts of tea leaves, coffee beans, and cacao beans. Of these, *Thea*—the botanical name of the tea plant—is consumed in the largest quantities and is the most healthful. Tea came from China, where its early history is unknown, and did not become an article of trade until the fifth century. It was recognized as having medicinal properties in China and Japan and was rated as a Divine Remedy in the early 13th century, when it cured a great Shogun of an almost fatal attack of overfeasting. Even now a nice cup of tea is the first thing we think of after indigestion.

When it is not too strong, tea is soothing, mildly stimulating, and warming. Its nourishment comes from the sugar and cream or milk that is put into it, and its diuretic virtues depend, in part, on the quantity we drink. The correct way to drink tea is without any additions, and not strong. To prepare it, pour boiling fresh water over the tea leaves in a warmed procelain tea pot and let them infuse for a few minutes before pouring.

A special blend of tea leaves was prepared by George Charlton of Charing Cross in London for Earl Grey, according to a secret formula. It was introduced to the public in 1836 and is still one of the great teas.

Tea should be stored in air-tight metal containers. Although the Chinese thought it should be stored a year before use, it is better when purchased frequently in small tins than in large quantities.

Tisanes and Herb Teas

ROSE HIP TEA

Rose hips are the red seed vessels that remain when the leaves of the Wild Briar Rose fall. They are dried, and a tea infused from them is red in color and slightly acid. It cannot possibly cure as many ills as was once believed, but it is slightly astringent and rich in Vitamin C.

CAMOMILE TEA

Wash ¼ cup fresh camomile flowers, or use 1 tablespoon dried, to 4 cups boiling water. Let stand for 5 minutes, strain, and serve. Sweeten with honey if desired.

SAGE TEA

Wash ¼ cup sage leaves, picked fresh from the stalks, and boil them with the thin outside rind of a lemon in 4 cups water for 30 minutes. Less sage is required if dried leaves are used.

PEPPERMINT TEA

Pour 2 cups boiling water over 2 teaspoons crushed peppermint leaves. Let the infusion draw for 10 minutes. Strain and serve.

LINDEN BLOSSOM TEA

The blossom of the linden, also called the lime tree, is dried to make the famous Tilleul on which the French have retired for generations. It is a digestive tonic and supposedly calming. Pour 2 cups boiling water over 1 tablespoon dried linden blossoms and let infuse for 5 minutes before straining.

Iced Tea Drinks

Tea has been iced and spiced and variously combined to make a most successful and cooling summer drink. It is enhanced with sprigs of mint, lemon slices, orange juice, and ginger ale. It can be sweetened with honey.

ICED TEA

2 quarts fresh water   1 lemon, thinly sliced
¼ cup black tea leaves

Use Earl Grey, Hookwah, Lapsang Souchong, Breakfast, or tea of your own choice.

Bring fresh water to a rolling boil and pour over the tea leaves all at once. Let the tea steep for exactly 3 minutes. Stir well and pour into a pitcher through a fine strainer. This method makes a clear tea. Long refrigeration or too-long steeping makes it cloudy. Let the pitcher cool and then put in a cool place. When ready to serve, pour the cool, uniced tea over ice cubes in tall glass. Add a lemon slice, and if it has to be sweetened, use a brown-sugar or raw-sugar syrup.

VARIATIONS

1. Add 2 teaspoons grated orange or lemon rind to the tea while it is steeping.

2. Sweeten with honey to taste instead of sugar. The honey may be stirred into the tea while it is still warm, or added after the tea is poured.

3. Pass small pitchers of orange, lemon, lime, and/or pineapple juice with the tea.

4. Put a few cloves into the tea while it is steeping.

Garnish with: Orange, lemon, or lime slices, sticks of pineapple, a cinnamon stick, or orange slices stuck with cloves. Or a sprig of mint, whole fresh strawberries, or curls of orange or lemon rind.

If black tea leaves are not available for iced tea, use 6 tea bags per quart of boiling water.

ICED TEA PUNCH

1 cup raw sugar
1 cup boiling water
3 cups very strong tea
3 cups orange juice
1 cup lemon juice

1 cup raspberry juice
1 cup juice pressed from a
    ripe pineapple
1 quart chilled soda or
    sparkling water

Boil sugar and water for just 5 minutes without stirring. Combine the syrup with the tea and fruit juices and chill until ready to serve. Pour over a block of ice in a punch bowl and add 1 quart soda.

FRUIT ICED TEA PUNCH

3 cups very strong tea
¾ cup raw sugar
1 cup lemon juice
2½ cups orange juice

2 cups pineapple juice
1 quart chilled ginger ale
2 oranges and 1 lemon, sliced
3 sprigs mint

Make the tea and stir in the sugar until it dissolves. As soon as the tea is cold, combine it with the fruit juices and chill until needed. Just before serving, add chilled ginger ale, fruit, and mint.

STRAWBERRY TEA PUNCH

4 cups strong tea
½ cup raw sugar
1 cup orange juice
½ cup lemon juice

3 cups pineapple juice
1 quart chilled ginger ale
1 pint basket strawberries,
    hulled

Pour the hot tea over the sugar and stir until dissolved. Add fruit juices and chill until needed. Just before serving, pour over a block of ice in a punch bowl and add the ginger ale and strawberries.

Dairy Drinks

One of the most important of all foods, *milk* is essential in the feeding of infants and children. When it is pasteurized, or pasteurized and homogenized, it is an almost perfect food. It contains protein, calcium, phosphorus, riboflavin, thiamin, and Vitamins A, B, C, and G. A great many American adults are milk drinkers although it is not essential after growth has been reached, but its byproduct, cheese, is a valuable part of healthful adult nutrition. An 8-ounce glass of whole milk contains 165 calories and about 12 grams of carbohydrates.

Buttermilk is more easily digested and contains 90 calories and 13 grams of carbohydrates per 8-ounce glass.

Properly *yogurt* should be sweet, not acid, and thick enough to cut with a spoon. It can also be thinned into a beverage. Yogurt in the United States is of semisolid consistency and acid in taste and can be bought sweetened and combined with fruits . . . which Turks deplore. One-half cup of plain yogurt contains about 65 calories and 7 grams of carbohydrates, and it rates as a natural health food. Millions of Turks eat yogurt or drink Ayran (thinned yogurt) every day of their lives. They cook with it and attribute their longevity to it. Yogurt contains lactic bacilli, which aid digestion.

How to Make Yogurt at Home

It is not necessary to buy the Bacillus Bulgaris to make yogurt. All that is needed is a few tablespoons of yogurt. The bacillus goes on breeding, and a small quantity retained from each day's supply will make the next. The ingredients are 1 quart fresh milk to about 2 tablespoons of yogurt. The process takes about 8 hours and requires an even temperature. With an electric yogurt-making machine to control the temperature, all that is necessary is to heat the milk to a boil and cool it to 109° F., stir in the retained yogurt, and pour it into the jars in the electrically heated appliance. Homemade yogurt is richer and smoother than the commercial product, and for special occasions it can be made with cream instead of milk.

Making yogurt without an electric yogurt heater is a matter of making a container in which the jars can be held without moving them at an even, warm temperature for 8 hours. The kitchen has to be 65° F. or over, and the jars have to be enclosed in an insulated and sealed container. Housewives in Turkey, who make yogurt every day, use nests of sacking or down-filled pillows that look like inverted tea cozys, but the climate is warm and they experiment until the insulation is heavy enough to hold the needed heat.

Yogurt is thinned with water to make Ayran or Mast, a healthy and refreshing beverage. Stir or blend about 2 cups yogurt to one cup cold water until smooth and thick. Change proportions to taste and chill the Ayran until needed. A little salt is added for nondieters.

How to Make Thick Milk and Devonshire Cream

Thick milk—Dicke Milch—is used in Europe as a food for children and an addition to fruits and desserts. Pour 1 quart pasteurized, but not homogenized, milk into a shallow pan in the evening and set it aside in a cool place until morning. Then move it gently to a warm place—on an asbestos pad on a very low burner, or the back of the stove. It must not simmer but should be warm for about one hour. Move again to a cool place and let stand for a day until it thickens. Thick milk must be moved gently and not stirred or disturbed until it is thick and ready to eat.

Devonshire Cream or Clotted Cream: pour 2 quarts pasteurized but not homogenized milk into the top of a large double broiler or deep pan so that it is about 8 inches deep. Set it aside in a cool place for 24 hours. Lift the pan gently to the stove and either set it over the lower section of a double boiler or over a saucepan of boiling water until the milk is heated to 175° F. Return to a cool place and after it is cold, skim off the cream with a skimmer.

Milk Drinks and Shakes

SESAME MILK

2 tablespoons broken Shredded Wheat	1 tablespoon honey, or to taste
1 tablespoon sesame seeds	¾ cup cold milk

Blend until smooth. Add light cream if mixture is too thick.

SOYBEAN MILK

1 cup soybeans	3 cups milk
4 cups water	1 tablespoon honey

Soak beans in water for 2 hours. Boil in the same water, stirring constantly, for 20 minutes. Cool slightly and pour the contents of the kettle into the blender in 3 batches and blend with milk and honey. Chill before serving.

MAPLE WHIP

1 cup maple syrup	⅔ cup heavy cream, whipped, OR
2 quarts cold milk	
2 teaspoons vanilla extract	6 small scoops homemade
¼ cup roughly chopped walnuts, optional	vanilla ice cream

In electric beater or blender, beat syrup, milk, and vanilla together for 1 minute. Pour into 6 glasses and chill for a few minutes. Garnish with whipped cream and chopped walnuts or float a small scoop of ice cream in each glass.

MAPLE NOG

3 eggs, well beaten ⅓ cup maple or brown sugar

½ teaspoon vanilla extract 1 teaspoon maple flavoring 6 cups cold milk

Beat eggs, sugar, vanilla, and maple flavoring until light and fluffy. Beat in the milk and chill before serving in 6 tall, chilled glasses.

EGGNOG FOR CHILDREN

3 cups cold milk   3 eggs
3 tablespoons honey

Blend all ingredients and serve.

MALTED EGGNOG FOR CHILDREN

2 eggs, beaten 1 teaspoon honey 3 tablespoons malted milk powder

1½ cups cold milk ½ teaspoon vanilla extract Grating of nutmeg

Beat eggs with honey and malted milk powder, add cold milk and vanilla, and beat until foamy. Pour into tall glasses and grate a little nutmeg over each. For a warm nog in winter, scald the milk and serve in handled mugs. Serves two.

ORANGE EGGNOG

2 cups fresh orange juice, cold 1 tablespoon honey

2 eggs 1 dash vanilla ½ cup light cream, cold

Pinch of cinnamon

Blend all ingredients until smooth, and pour into chilled glasses and serve with a sprig of mint.

HOMEMADE ICE CREAM SODAS

2 cups crushed fresh or
  stewed fruit
1½ cups cold milk

6 small scoops homemade
  ice cream
1 pint chilled soda, ginger
  ale, or sparkling water

Divide fruit over 6 tall glasses. Add ¼ cup milk to each. Add a scoop of ice cream to each glass and fill with sparkling water. Stir once and serve with spoon and straws.

MILK SHAKES

3 cups cold milk
3 tablespoons thin honey
2 cups fresh cold fruit

1 tray very cold ice cubes,
  cracked or crushed

Pit or core fresh fruit and cut into rough dice. Use peaches, apricots, apples, strawberries, or any fruit except melons. Put 1 cup milk with 1 tablespoon honey and ⅔ cup fruit into blender with 6 crushed ice cubes. Blend until frappéed. Pour into tall, cold glasses and make two more batches.

PEACHES, PLUMS, AND CREAM

3 to 4 fresh ripe peaches,
  pitted and roughly
  sliced
4 to 6 fresh ripe red plums,
  pitted and quartered

1 cup brown sugar
1 cup light cream
¼ cup lemon juice
1 cup crushed ice

Pit and prepare fruit for blender. There should be enough to make 1 cup each. Blend fruit with sugar, cream, lemon juice, and ice and blend until smooth. Serve in 6 chilled glasses.

ORANGE YOGURT

3 oranges, peeled and
sectioned
Outside rind of 1 of the
oranges
1 tablespoon brown
sugar

3 egg yolks
1 tablespoon honey, or to
taste
3 cups homemade yogurt
1 sprinkling of powdered
ginger

Cut the outside rind from one of the oranges with a potato peeler and cut into short lengths. Puree the orange sections, rind, and sugar in the blender. Add yolks and honey and when the mixture is smooth add yogurt. Chill until needed. Pour the mixture into chilled glasses and add a little powdered ginger to the top of each.

STRAWBERRY COOLER

1 quart strawberries
hulled
3 cups cold milk
½ cup thin honey

1 tablespoon lemon juice
1 cup heavy cream
3 tablespoons chopped
walnuts

Clean the strawberries and set the 6 largest aside. Blend or sieve the rest with milk, honey, lemon juice, and half the cream and blend or beat until smooth. Chill well. Whip the remaining cream. Serve in tall, chilled glasses with a topping of whipped cream. Put a strawberry on each and a sprinkling of walnuts.

CHAPTER VII

Dieting and the Maintenance of Good Health

A diet is the food and drink we consume considered in terms of its effect on our health. It is usually a particular selection of foods that has been prescribed to improve or cure an existing physical condition. Since overweight is a common and detrimental physical condition (from which 60 percent of all Americans over 40 years of age are suffering) we usually think of a diet as meaning a temporary reduction of food for purposes of weight loss.

A *crash diet* is supposed to accomplish this loss of weight in a specified number of days. Most of the crash diets achieve just that, but the decisive problem in all dieting is whether the successful weight loss can be maintained. After most crash diets the weight returns in a discouragingly short time.

Dietetics is the science concerned with nutritional planning and the preparation of healthful meals. A *dietician* has studied dietetics and practices it professionally.

229

A *regimen* is much the same as a diet, but we think of it as a prevailing rule for life rather than as a short or drastic attempt to cure a condition. Going onto a healthful regimen is a long-term undertaking, but it is the most painless, the surest, safest, and easiest way of losing weight and keeping it off permanently. Diets and crash diets are not forever, but a common-sense regimen is.

Anyone wanting to lose weight must understand that the eating habits that put on the fat (gradually over a period of years) will do so again after we go back to them. Pounds invariably return faster than they came off and faster than they accumulated originally. Ergo . . . a decision to lose weight does not mean just a few weeks of deprivations, it means a departure—without return—from the way we have been eating. It does not mean starvation or pangs of hunger, but it does mean a whole new approach to our daily meals.

Unfortunately a sensible, healthful regimen that will permanently adjust overweight will not do it in a few days. The years of steady incorrect eating that built up the superfluous fat cannot be undone with a ten-day crash diet. In the majority of cases, overweight is the result of the quantity and quality of the food we ate and the circumstances under which we ate it, and only a change from these conditions can bring about a loss of undesirable fat.

One of the most important factors in losing weight is psychological. Unless there is a relatively rapid initial weight loss—even though it does not mean a loss of actual fat—patients are discouraged. This is especially true where various diets have been tried without lasting success. Proving that they too can lose weight encourages dieters to find the strength needed to switch over to a common-sense weight-loss regimen. For this reason it is sometimes advisable to start with a drastic diet, not for a few crash days, but as the beginning of the long, slow adjustment to healthful eating and the consequent return to normal weight.

There are several methods for quick weight reduction to which we will return. The regimen for healthful eating is not a set daily schedule, but rather a group of simple rules. Eating healthfully means applying these rules, but until such time as unnecessary weight has been lost, the rules should not be broken and the program should be firmly adhered to.

The Twelve Weight Loss Rules

1. Eat three times a day and eat *nothing* between meals. The smallest "bite" not only adds calories, it arouses feelings of hunger.

2. Eat only until hunger is satisfied at each meal, even though there may be food left on your plate or another course to follow. Try to recognize the moment when you are no longer hungry and stop eating as soon as you reach it.

3. Drink liquids only between meals. While losing weight, drink only fresh water, weak tea, or herbal teas. Quantities should be determined by your doctor.

4. With the exception of homemade consommé, bouillon, or vegetable stock, in small quantities, cut out all soups.

5. *Never forget to eat slowly and chew well.* These are ways of satisfying a feeling of hunger.

6. Cut all visible fat from the meat and poultry you eat.

7. Do not go back to sleep after breakfast. Do not nap or have a little siesta after luncheon and do not go to bed immediately after the evening meal.

8. Reduce salt in cooking and do not salt at the table. Learn to use herbs rather than seasonings to improve flavor.

9. As far as possible, take regular exercise, walk, do gymnastic exercises, or take an active part in a suitable sport.

10. Weigh yourself once a week, at the same time of day under the same conditions. Keep a record.

11. Unless you are instituting *chicken days* or *fruit days* (when only one food is eaten) always see to it that your menu is varied.

12. Always eat your meals according to the healthful eating rotation mentioned in Chapter I.

The Six Healthful Eating Rules

1. Eat whole fruit and do not drink fruit juices.

2. Eat fruit about 20 minutes before the meal, start the meal with a fruit salad, and follow with a vegetable.

3. Half of your daily food must consist of fresh fruits and vegetables, and half the fruits and vegetables must be eaten raw. Furthermore they must be eaten *before* the other foods.

4. The other half of your daily food should consist of lean meats, poultry, fish, eggs, dark breads, and cheese.

5. Do not ever eat when you are in a hurry, under tension, or nervous.

6. If you gain weight, always cut back to a very lean and limited regimen until it is lost. Do not let it stay on and do not let it accumulate. A series of dinner invitations or a few weeks of travel may put on pounds . . . get them off quickly before they settle in again.

By combining the 12 weight loss rules and the 6 healthful eating rules, a pattern for losing weight will emerge. Follow the following list of *permitted* and *prohibited* foods until the weight is lost. After that abide by the general healthful eating regimen.

While losing weight avoid:

Dried fruits such as
  apricots and prunes
Dried vegetables such as
  lentils, baked beans,
  dried peas
All sweets
All alcohol
Fat meats such as pork

All sausages and luncheon
  meats
Turkey, duck, goose, and fat
  fowls
All rice, pastas, white breads,
  pastries, pies, cakes, and
  crackers
Spices and condiments

Smoked fish such as sardines

All of the above looks like the same old list of *don'ts*, but there is a great difference. By changing the rotation of the courses, the appetite is usually satisfied before or during the meat course, and the craving for bread, desserts, and beverages disappears completely.

The permitted foods are:

Skim milk
Buttermilk
Yogurt
Low-fat cheeses such as
  Edam
Low-fat cottage cheese
Lean beef
Veal
Chicken
Venison
Liver
Kidneys
Tongue
Cod
Trout
Flounder
Pike
Sole and all the lean fish
Eggs—from 4 to 7 a
  week

Diet margarine for spread
Butter for spread
Corn oil, sunflower oil,
  safflower oil, peanut or
  linseed oil for cooking
Whole-grain, whole-
  wheat, and sprouted-
  wheat breads, graham
  crackers, and rye crisps,
  pumpernickel, Scandi-
  navian thin breads,
  Waerland bread, and
  home-baked dark breads
Boiled or baked potatoes
All *fresh* vegetables
All *fresh* fruit and berries
All teas and herb teas
Mineral waters and
  sparkling water
All herbs

The permitted food preparations are:

Broiling, boiling, pan broiling, and grilling
Simmering, steaming, and poaching
Baking and roasting

The *prohibited* food preparations are:

All frying in shallow or deep fats, all breading or batter frying, and all preparations that require dredging

The Single-Food Days

You can have *milk, cottage cheese,* and *fruit days.* Some dieters pin their faith on *juice days,* but the most satisfactory is the *chicken day.* Buy a 2½- to 2¾-pound broiler and plan to eat half of it on your *total chicken day.*

Chicken Day

BREAKFAST:
   1 soft-boiled egg
   1 piece wheat crisp or whole-wheat toast
   Tea with lemon, without sugar

30 MINUTES BEFORE LUNCHEON:
   ½ grapefruit

LUNCHEON:
   1 tomato
   Lettuce salad with a dressing based on lemon juice and ½ tablespoon sunflower or safflower oil
   ¼ broiled chicken (use rotisserie, if possible, for butterless broiling)

DINNER:
   Apple, lettuce, and celery salad
   ¼ broiled chicken
   Tea with lemon, without sugar

BEFORE RETIRING:

1 orange

Repeat this day twice a week.

Vegetable Day

BREAKFAST:

Herb tea, camomile, or peppermint tea
1 slice whole-grain bread
1 tomato
2 tablespoons herbed cottage cheese

LUNCHEON:

Steamed fresh vegetables, depending on the season of year. In spring and summer eat about 10 ounces tender spring vegetables. Prepare them without salt, with fresh or dried herbs, and with a little fresh butter.

30 MINUTES BEFORE DINNER:

1 apple

DINNER:

Raw vegetables in a salad, such as tomato,
cucumber, lettuce
10 ounces steamed vegetables
1 very small steamed potato
2 pieces rye crisp, optional
Tea with lemon and without sugar

Repeat this day twice a week.

Other Diet Days

I

BREAKFAST:
  ½ grapefruit or 1 orange
  Tea or herb tea without sugar
  1 slice whole-grain toast
  2 tablespoons herbed cottage cheese

30 MINUTES BEFORE LUNCHEON:
  1 apple or orange

LUNCHEON:
  Mixed raw vegetable salad
  1 steamed vegetable
  1 small portion of broiled meat, steak, hamburger,
  or chop, all visible fat removed
  1 small steamed potato

30 MINUTES BEFORE DINNER:
  Fruit, depending on the season

DINNER:
  Tomato, egg, and lettuce salad
  1 steamed vegetable

BEFORE RETIRING:
  1 orange

II

BREAKFAST:
  1 orange or berries
  1 soft-boiled or poached egg
  1 slice whole-grain toast, lightly buttered
  Tea without sugar

30 MINUTES BEFORE LUNCHEON:
  ½ grapefruit or 1 apple

LUNCHEON:

Cauliflower vinaigrette
1 cup bouillon with 1 envelope gelatin and parsley
2 rye crisps or whole-wheat thins

30 MINUTES BEFORE DINNER:

Apple and orange salad

DINNER:

Poached egg on spinach
1 slice Edam cheese with a small cluster of grapes

BEFORE RETIRING:

1 orange

III

BREAKFAST:

Fresh fruit in season
1 glass buttermilk
1 slice sprouted-wheat bread, lightly buttered

30 MINUTES BEFORE LUNCHEON:

1 pear

LUNCHEON:

Salad of raw vegetables
1 portion beef or veal, all visible fat removed

30 MINUTES BEFORE DINNER:

1 tangerine or fruit in season

DINNER:

Chef's salad with a julienne of cheese and
chicken, hard-cooked egg, and raw vegetables
2 slices of whole-wheat toast
¼ cantaloupe

BEFORE RETIRING:

1 orange

IV

BREAKFAST:

Fresh fruit in season
1 poached egg
2 pieces whole-wheat toast
2 tablespoons herbed cottage cheese

30 MINUTES BEFORE LUNCHEON:

Orange and grapefruit sections

LUNCHEON:

Raw mushroom, raw zucchini, and endive salad
1 poached fillet of sole
1 small new potato, steamed

30 MINUTES BEFORE DINNER:

1 apple

DINNER:

Sliced herbed tomatoes and watercress salad
Cottage cheese
Seedless grapes
Pumpernickel

Eat all you want of raw and cooked fresh vegetables and fresh fruit. They supply necessary vitamins and minerals. Eat all other items on the menus according to what is considered one normal portion, page 48. If hunger is appeased before the suggested menu is eaten, STOP EATING. If necessary, decrease the size of the portions at future meals, but do not decrease the variety of the food.

Reduction Rate

If you have 10 to 12 pounds of fat to lose, or if you are just beginning to put on weight, you can reduce by going on the above diet. It will take about one week before an actual weight loss will show and about two to three more weeks to get the rest off. The regimen should be adhered to for at least another four to six weeks before you can safely add a few items. After that it is a matter of watching the scales and *always remaining on the common-sense health regimen* as outlined in Chapter I. If weight goes up, return to the above diet at once. If it remains the same, then eat the same. If you continue to lose a little, add a few more items . . . another slice of sprouted-wheat bread, another teaspoon of butter. If you have more than 15 pounds to lose, or if you are under medical treatment for any reason whatever, see your physician before you go on any diet.

Do not use diet pills or artificial sweeteners. Do not starve yourself. You are learning to eat naturally and healthfully, and weight should be lost naturally and healthfully. We are recommending the framework of a common-sense regimen with which to regain and maintain health. It is only because general well-being depends to a great extent on weight, that the regimen should be pared down for faster weight loss at first. When overweight is lost, follow the regimen with all the recipe variations in Chapter VI. Healthful eating will ultimately adjust the imbalance that caused the gain in weight by satisfying the feelings of hunger early in the meal. The limited regimen for quicker weight loss is only suggested to encourage the easily discouraged loser during the first three weeks of healthful eating.

When we are faced with an important change in our habitual food regimen, the important thing is to make the new regimen as attractive as possible. Most sufferers from overweight have neglected fruits and vegetables, and the only way to make them more tempting is to prepare them in new ways. The salad and vegetable recipes illustrate how much more we can do with them than we did in the past.

Permanent weight loss must be undertaken in three steps. First a quick initial loss for encouragement; next, a limited healthful eating regimen used as a temporary diet until the weight is lost; and last, by following the regular healthful eating regimen to keep the weight off permanently.

How to Go About the Quick Initial Loss of Weight

While crash diets are useless when the users return to their regular eating habits, some of them are an excellent means of encouragement at the beginning of a serious healthful eating and reducing program. A few wise ideas can be picked up by checking the methods of reduction at the famous spas, baths, watering towns, and health resorts of the world. In these places the doctors are constantly confronted with weight problems. Since overweight is now recognized as a threat to health and since it can contribute to serious conditions, it must be looked upon as an illness—in some cases it can even develop into a fatal illness. Of all the serious illnesses, it is the one we take most lightly, and the only one we do not treat as an illness at all. No one calls the office to say they will be out for a few days due to a serious case of overweight . . . but that is exactly what they should do. Nothing starts a reducing diet off as well as a few days in bed on an extremely lean diet.

We are told that most illnesses are only recognizable after the symptoms have become obvious—which is usually after the illness is in an advanced stage. Just so with fat. It settles in long before it appears on the surface and actually distorts the figure. It takes about 20 years of rigid adherence to the wrong foods and to too many of them to develop a serious overweight problem and obesity. Doctors often recommend drastic measures to reverse the processes. Where serious weight loss is important your physician will advise. For minor but equally essential weight loss the recommendations are often a laxative, or a fruit or juice day to begin with. The most important thing is to clear the decks. Accept and issue no invitations, do not eat at restaurants or travel. Do not think you can accompany your friends or follow your regular routine without being tempted away from the schedule. Devote the first few days, after the decision is made, to staying away from all temptation and thinking and talking about your diet plans as little as possible.

Losing weight is a *do-it-yourself* undertaking. No one can do it for you, and all claims that fat can be massaged, rolled, baked, or pummeled off are false. The only way to get fat off is to eat it off, and the best way to do that is alone and silently, without long discussions and *without complaint.*

Some of the weight-loss methods are based on group psychology. You can watch your own weight at home, but in a group you watch each other's weight, and this lends great strength and impetus to some personalities. The idea that we all lose together when we lose is good, but basically losing weight is a personal and lonely occupation, and it is far better to discuss it after than before the fact.

One of the greatest helps in making the decisive decision is taking a long look at yourself. Do not look at yourself in the pose you always assume (half turned and holding your breath) when you know you are going to see yourself in your own flattering mirror. Look at your reflection in an unflattering, cruel light, as you can see it in a dark shop window as you pass by on the street. Look at yourself in profile and you will wonder where the you who used to wear a size 12 and dance all night can be in that blurred outline.

What many Americans think of as the horrors of aging . . . feeling unwanted with aches and pains and shortness of breath . . . is actually the pandemic national disease of fat.

The Reasons We Gain Weight

The obvious reasons for putting on weight are usually *overeating* and *underexercising*. All other causes for putting on excess fat should be treated by a physician. The reasons for overeating and underexercising are many, ranging from habit, suggestion, and unhappiness to the circumstances of our lives, to age, and to the constant temptations which are placed before us. Our professions often impose frequent entertaining, sedentary occupations, and no time for regular exercise.

One of the great handicaps to following a sensible food regimen is the geographical layout of our homes. Today's homes are different from our grandparents' homes because our lives are totally different. The distances are shorter and the spaces are smaller. We are no longer three storeys away from the larder, and the icebox is no longer guarded by a formidable cook. The full refrigerator and our food supplies are right there, a constant temptation as we pass by. It is hard to go through our kitchens twenty times a day without stopping for one of those long, aimless looks into the refrigerator. They can result in our eating anything from a cup of custard to an enormous turkey drumstick. Most of us do what the westerners call "piecing" and what we used to call "raiding the icebox." And we wonder why we gain weight at home and feel better when we are away from home. We also wonder why our husbands, who eat large luncheons with desserts, not to mention coffee breaks with pastries, manage to stay thin longer than we do.

The housewife, all innocently, also participates in her children's meals. If children are young enough to eat separately, their mother inevitably gets her between-meal snacks without thinking about it. She is bound to finish the last quarter of the perfectly good sandwich, or she tastes the corner of the bread and honey. Usually she cannot bear to throw away the second half of the orange or the last of the cereal. The secret of how to put on weight is to eat often and little, and while the average housewife does not realize it, that is exactly what she is doing . . . with predictable results. Most mothers of young children are following a full-scale "often-and-little" regimen, guaranteed to add weight, discomfort and, as a result, poorer health.

The secret of food manufacturers' advertising campaigns is to show you food in full and tempting color. Having a centrally located and easily available kitchen does just that. Going there to prepare the children's meals shows you food and makes you hungry. The answer is to prepare the exact amount of food your children require and no more than they will eat. Butter one slice of bread instead of two, select small bananas instead of large ones, cook half the oatmeal and *don't share it* (always remember it is much better for them than for you).

As far as the beautifully stocked and irresistible refrigerator is concerned, simply put a container of crisp celery stalks and carrot sticks near the front. Whenever you just inadvertently *happen* to open the door, take one of these instead of a slab of last night's ham.

A healthful food regimen can include some piecing, but *always as a substitute, never as a supplement.*

There are a lot of unpleasant truths about overweight that have to be faced. All of them interlock with healthful eating and will hopefully convince you that *healthful eating is healthful undereating* and that 99 times out of 100, unhealthful eating is overeating.

A switchover to a healthful eating regimen for life will mean that fat will never raise those ugly numbers on the scales again. And beside all the good medical reasons, being thin will mean feeling and looking younger.

Losing weight is *not* a crash project so that you can get back into that size 14 dress. It is *not* something to do quickly so that you will look devastating on the beach next July. It is, in most cases, a serious decision to take a long step toward a more comfortable, happier, healthier, and better-looking life.

Think of overweight in terms of a woman condemned to carrying a 40-pound package wherever she goes, upstairs, downstairs, all around with her every day. Our instant reaction is that she is going to overstrain her heart. If we saw a man carrying a 60-pound package up a hill on a hot day, we would think he was abusing his heart. The only difference is in the location of the weight and in the ease with which it can be dropped. They could drop their packages and unburden their hearts, but they cannot drop fat without effort and strength of mind. Doing it with a healthful regimen is easier because it lessens the appetite from the beginning.

A woman who was just old enough to see a diet looming in her future asked me about healthful eating. Before I had gotten very far she asked about her daily ice-cold cocktail.

When I told her that there should not be any, she said, "You've lost me," and turned away.

Most people have established eating and drinking habits that a healthful regimen is bound to interfere with at some point. Asking an adult to make a complete change would most often be a hopeless task. "You've lost me" may come with the cocktail or the dessert, but it is bound to come at some point with everyone.

I am aware that there are coffee drinkers who could not possibly switch to herb teas and total beefeaters who would not want to switch to several vegetables at each meal—but even a small step toward common-sense, down-to-earth eating is beneficial. No one should consider that he has been lost.

Do not uproot your lives, make some gradual changes: eat a little less, eat slower, start by giving up canned and processed foods. But do not reject the plan to eat more healthfully because you do not want to give up your occasional chocolate sundae.

Weight and Height Chart for Children 1 to 12 Years Old

GIRLS:

Age	Height in Inches	Pounds Weight
1	29¼–31¼	21½–23¾
2	34–35½	26¼–28¼
3	37½–40¼	30½–34
4	40¾–42¾	34½–37
5	43–45	38½–43
6	45½–47	44–48
7	47½–49	49–52
8	49½–51	54½–58
9	51¼–52¾	61–62
10	53¼–54½	63–68
11	55¼–57	70–75
12	57¼–59¼	78–86

BOYS:

Age	Height in Inches	Pounds Weight
1	29¾–31¾	22¼–24½
2	34½–36	26–29
3	38–40¾	31–35
4	41¼–43	35½–39
5	43¾–45½	40¼–44
6	46–47½	45–48
7	48–49¼	49–53¼
8	50–51¼	55–58½
9	52–53¼	60–64
10	54–54½	66–69
11	55¼–56¾	71–75
12	57–58¾	77–82

Weight and Height Chart for Men
Ages 25 and Over *

HEIGHT (with shoes) Feet	Inches	Small Frame	Medium Frame	Large Frame
5	2	112–120	118–129	126–141
5	3	115–123	121–133	129–144
5	4	118–126	124–136	132–148
5	5	121–129	127–139	135–152
5	6	124–133	130–143	138–156
5	7	128–137	134–147	142–161
5	8	132–141	138–152	147–166
5	9	136–145	142–156	151–170
5	10	140–150	146–160	155–174
5	11	144–154	150–165	159–179
6	0	148–158	154–170	164–184
6	1	152–162	158–175	168–189
6	2	156–167	162–180	173–194
6	3	160–171	167–185	178–199
6	4	164–175	172–190	182–204

* Courtesy of the Metropolitan Life Insurance Company.

Weight and Height Chart for Women Ages 25 and Over *

HEIGHT (with 2-inch heels) Feet	Inches	Small Frame	Medium Frame	Large Frame
4	10	92–98	96–107	104–119
4	11	94–101	98–110	106–122
5	0	96–104	101–113	109–125
5	1	99–107	104–116	112–128
5	2	102–110	107–119	115–131
5	3	105–113	110–122	118–134
5	4	108–116	113–126	121–138
5	5	111–119	116–130	125–142
5	6	114–123	120–135	129–146
5	7	118–127	124–139	133–150
5	8	122–131	128–143	137–154
5	9	126–135	132–147	141–158
5	10	130–140	136–151	145–163
5	11	134–144	140–155	149–168
6	0	138–148	144–159	153–173

For girls between 18 and 25, subtract 1 pound for each year under 25.

* Courtesy of the Metropolitan Life Insurance Company.

MAIL ORDER LIST

Maison Glass
52 East 58 Street
New York, N.Y. 10022
Telephone: (212) PL5-3316-7-8
For the best in domestic and imported delicacies with an excellent line of health foods, bread, oils, honey, sugars, salts, dried fruits, cereals, teas, dietetic jams, fruit vinegars, dried mushrooms and herbs, farinaceous foods, and cheeses. Mail orders are given special attention and usually shipped the same day. Minimum order $10.00.

Panacea Corporation
323 Third Avenue (between 24 and 25 Streets)
New York, N.Y. 10010
Telephone: (212) 725-2320
A large natural-food and herb store. Organic fruits and vegetables, salt-free products, flours, breads. Appliances, yogurt makers, and sprouters. Minimum mail order $5.00.

Alexander's
731 Lexington Avenue (between 58 and 59 Streets)
New York, N.Y. 10022
Telephone: (212) 593-0880
A large and very well-stocked health-food department.

Brownies
19 East 16 Street
New York, N.Y. 10003
Telephone: (212) AL5-2838
Large, well-stocked health-food store. Home-baked breads and cakes, nut butters, vegetables, and fruits.

Sears, Roebuck & Co.
Health-food products are not available at their stores but can be mail ordered. Send for *The Naturama Catalogue* (39K7310), Sears, Roebuck & Co., Dept. 139 K, 925 S. Homan Avenue, Chicago, Illinois 60607.

The Good Earth
1336 First Avenue
New York, N.Y. 10021
Telephone: (212) BU8-7408
One of the best of the health-food stores, with a wide assortment. Carries a complete line of recognized brands as well as products packed by their own Organic Farms.

Mr. Dunderbak's
76 Street and First Avenue
New York, N.Y. 10021
Telephone: YU8-5410
Not a health-food store but a well-supplied gourmet shop specializing in fresh fruit juices, biscuits, thin breads, and cheeses.

For stone-ground flours and cornmeal:

Old Sturbridge Village
Wight Grist Mill Products
Sturbridge, Massachusetts
(Also available at the Publick House in Sturbridge)
Mail-order blanks will be sent on request for Grist Mill Products: yellow or white cornmeal, whole-wheat flour, graham flour, rye and buckwheat flours, brown-bread mix and cracked-wheat cereal.

Old Grist Mill Flours
Clarks Falls Grist Mill
Clarks Falls
North Stonington, Connecticut

INDEX

251